COMBAT ARMS

## MODERN

# CARRIERS

Edited by BILL GUNSTON

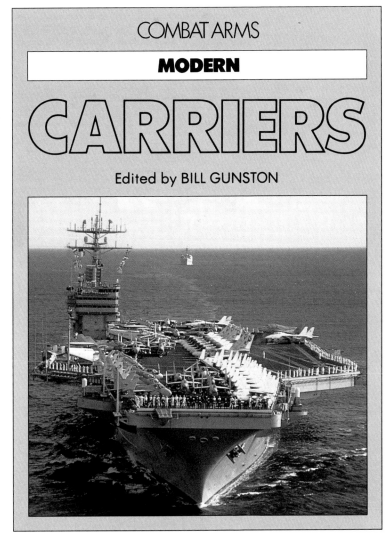

a Salamander book

Published by Salamander Books Limited
LONDON • NEW YORK

# A Salamander Book

Published by
Salamander Books Ltd.,
52 Bedford Row,
London WC1R 4LR,
United Kingdom.

© Salamander Books Ltd. 1988

ISBN 086101 414 6

Distributed in the United Kingdom by
Hodder & Stoughton Services,
PO Box 6, Mill Road,
Dunton Green, Sevenoaks,
Kent TN13 2XX.

All correspondence concerning the content of
this volume should be addressed to the publisher.

# Credits

**Project Manager:** Ray Bonds
**Designers:** Paul Johnson, Roger Hyde
**Colour artwork:** © Salamander
Books Ltd.
**Ship outlines:** © John Jordan
**Filmset** by The Old Mill
**Colour reproduction:** Kentscan Ltd.
**Printed** in Belgium by Proost International
Book Production, Turnhout.

# Acknowledgments

**Bill Gunston** is a highly respected defense journalist who has
contributed to many international military journals. He is the
author of numerous volumes on defense subjects and is also
Assistant Compiler of *Jane's All The World's Aircraft.*

The publishers are indebted to David and Chris Miller for their
extensive contributions to this work.

**David Miller** is a serving British Officer whose career has taken
him to Singapore, Malaysia, the Mediterranean countries, and
the Falkland Islands. He is a regular contributor to international
defence publications, and author of many books on military
affairs.

**Chris Miller** is a former lieutenant in the Royal Navy. His career
included appointments to anti-submarine frigates, and to the
staff of a flag officer at one of the main NATO maritime
headquarters.

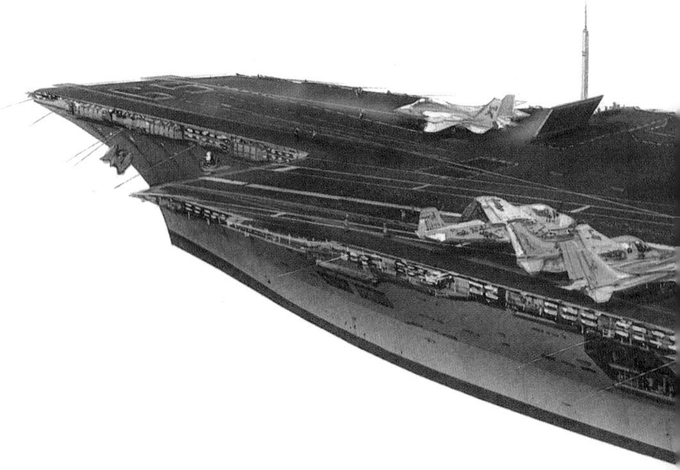

# Contents

THE AIRCRAFT carrier is the capital ship without parallel on today's oceans. Admiral of the Fleet Lord Hill-Norton, former British Chief of the Defence Staff, recently described it thus: "The Fleet Carrier — the most impressive fighting machine the world has ever seen. This one ship can unleash a greater variety of lethal weapons with a greater destructive power, at longer range, than any man-of-war in history."

The modern American carriers, with command centres rivalling those ashore, are capable of launching nuclear strikes and, with 90 of the very latest types of aircraft, have an air capability greater than that of all but the most sophisticated land-based air forces.

For many years the Western navies have dominated the aircraft carrier scene, with the US Navy maintaining a fleet of ever larger units, although the once significant British carrier force has dwindled away to almost nothing. The French maintain a two-carrier force but, these apart, there are a number of small (mostly ex-British) carriers scattered around the more sophisticated of the second-level navies.

Meanwhile, until recently, the Soviets, with no tradition of naval airpower, had nothing, despite the evidence from their writings that they considered the threat from nuclear-armed, carrier-borne aircraft to be of great significance to the Russian homeland, and numerous ship and submarine classes and weapons systems were developed to counter it. The Soviets themselves seem to have felt little need for carriers as their maritime ambitions apparently had not extended to blue-water power politics. But that position has dramatically changed and they are now posing an ever-growing threat to the West at sea. The late Admiral Gorshkov is on record as saying that: "The Soviet Navy will no longer be confined to its home waters, but will exploit the freedom of the seas and through its global presence in peacetime will spread Communist influence outside the borders of the USSR. Sea Power without Air Power is senseless."

## V/STOL less expensive

As in other naval spheres the cost of aircraft carriers is escalating rapidly; the next two US carriers of the Nimitz class will cost well over $2,000 million each for the ships alone, without the cost of the air wing. A number of navies have therefore been looking for a cheaper way to take airpower to sea, and in this the V/STOL (vertical/short takeoff and landing) aircraft seems to offer the only realistic answer.

There are currently four types of aircraft carrier. At the top end is the CTOL carrier (conventional take-off and landing), of which current examples range from the mighty American CVNs of 89,600 tons displacement down to the elderly carriers of about 20,000 tons in use in some navies.

Above: A fine portrait of HMS Ark Royal, third and last of the Royal Navy's so-called "through-deck cruisers", taken before fitting the Phalanx rapid-fire CIWS (Close-In Weapon System). CIWS was obviously needed; these costly ships were previously almost defenceless against aircraft or anti-ship missiles at close ranges.

These ships operate air wings of a size proportional to the tonnage, and usually in a mix of strike, air defence, patrol and ASW types.

The giants of the current carriers are the US Navy's Nimitz class, each capable of carrying up to 85 aircraft. These will be countered by the new Soviet CVN of some 75,000 tons full load displacement, which is due for sea trials by the end of the decade. But the Soviet Navy is unlikely to be able to match the US Navy in number for perhaps 40 to 50

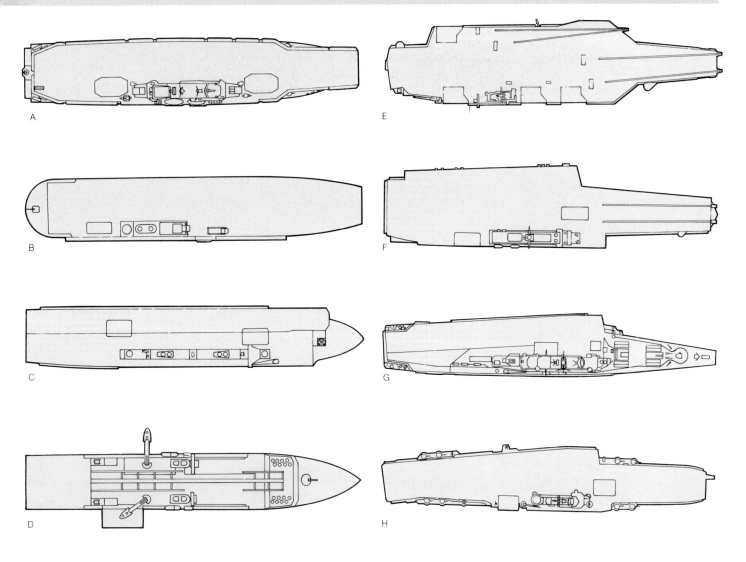

A

B

C

D

E

F

G

H

*Above: Plan views of modern carriers, A, Italian* Giuseppe Garibaldi; *B, Spanish* Principe de Asturias *(not yet showing the definitive armament fit); C, British* Invincible *class (not showing Phalanx CIWS); and D, the simple ship of about 5,800 tons proposed by Vosper Thorneycroft with two BAe SkyHooks for Sea Harriers.*

*Above: Plan views of four further modern carriers, again not to a common scale: E, USS* Nimitz *class; F, the large Soviet carrier (believed to be named* Kremlin *or* possibly Brezhnyev), *in general form but still highly provisional; G, Soviet Kiev class (except for the fourth ship,* Baku); *and H, French* Clemenceau *and* Foch.

years. The French Navy is firmly committed to two new nuclear-powered carriers of some 50,000 tons (PAH-1, 2), but no other navies are known to have plans for CVNs at this time.

Second come the new medium-sized carrier with full-length flight-decks, but which operate the V/STOL Sea Harrier or Yak-38 "Forger", together with large numbers of helicopters. These range in size from the Spanish *Principe de Asturias* (14,700 tons) to the British Invincible class (19,500 tons), with the Soviet Kiev class (42,000 tons) at the top end.

Similar in concept to these, but with a different primary purpose, are the third type — the amphibious assault ships, which have a large straight-through flight-deck for V/STOL aircraft and helicopters, but which also carry large marine forces (usually a battalion group). Typical of this group is the US Navy's Tarawa class (39,300 tons), which can carry up to 19 of the huge CH-53 Sea Stallion helicopters, together with some 1,700 troops.

Fourth comes a small group of ships in the 8,000 to 20,000 tons category with half-length flight-decks aft for operating helicopters, or possibly AV-8A/C Harriers, operating in the VTOL mode. There are also the ever growing number of small warships with a stern flight-deck for one or two, usually ASW, helicopters.

The future of the large nuclear-powered supercarrier seems assured in the US and Soviet navies, with the Americans planning for a fleet of 15 and the USSR for at least two, and probably many more. These large carriers are certainly very impressive and carry significant air power; they are also extremely effective command, communications and control ($C^3$) centres. But they are also massively expensive and, despite their air wing, on-board armament and protective escorts, they are still vulnerable. They are certainly prime targets for submarine attacks, and could well also be targeted by land-based long-range missiles.

The British Royal Navy's experience with CVA-01 has shown that designs can become too expensive, and that the cost of large carriers, plus the concomitant cost of the specialised aircraft for the air wing, can exceed the budget. It would appear then that technology will be applied to producing much cheaper carriers, thus enabling more effective and more survivable carriers to join the smaller navies — and perhaps the larger navies, too.

For the air component of carrier fleets it seems there are two major areas for development. First is the yet more effective and capable V/STOL aircraft, and the second is the development of a viable fleet airborne AEW platform, which does not need a large CTOL aircraft carrier.

## Flight-deck design

The design of the flight-deck is obviously crucial to the efficient operation of a carrier. In this a number of innovations have played a vital role since the advent of the turbojet-powered aircraft, including the angled flight-deck, automated approach and landing aids, and the steam catapult. Further improvements, such as deck-edge lifts, represent sensible, evolutionary steps to increase usable deck areas. The abortive British CVA-01 design, although conceived in the 1960s, still probably represents the ultimate arrangement for economical and efficient use of deck-space.

The alternative approach is the straight-through flight-deck, but this is now only suitable for V/STOL aircraft. In this the major breakthrough has been the invention (by Commander Douglas Taylor, RN) of the "ski-jump", which like so many great inventions is cheap and truly simple. Not only is the jump very easy to construct, but no modifications whatsoever are required for the aircraft, while the pilots find it safe and simple to use. Ski-jumps have already been fitted to the British carriers *Hermes* (12°), *Invincible* (7°), *Illustrious* (7°) and *Ark Royal* (12°), and to the Spanish *Principe de Asturias*. The US Marine Corps has bought three ramps for

*Right: The rear part of the superstructure of Minsk, second of the Soviet Kiev class of multirole "anti-submarine crusiers". These are among the most powerful warships in history, though they lack the capability of operating CTOL fixed-wing aircraft. Immediately aft of the large funnel uptake is one of the two illuminating and tracking radars (called "Head Light" by NATO) for the N-3 SAMs, surmounted by twin "Pop Group" radars for the N-4 SAMs. Next comes the rear "Owl Screech" radar to direct the aft 76mm guns, followed by the rear N-3 SAM launcher (unloaded).*

*Below right: One half of the Soviet carrier Kiev's ESM fit comprises two "Rum Tub" ESM antennas, two "Bell Bash" jammer antennas (below the top pair of "Side Globes") and two "Bell Thump" jammers (below the second pair of "Side Globes"), as on the Minsk.*

*Far right: ESM fit on Novorossiysk comprises "Rum Tub", "Bell Bash" and "Bell Thump". "Side Globe" is not fitted though its function is still performed by a different system. At the foot of the diagram is the "Tin Man" optronic device replacing "Tee Plinth" on Kiev (left).*

*Left: Derived from the UK-60A Black Hawk troop carrier of the US Army, the Sikorsky SH-60B Seahawk is the new ASW and anti-ship targeting helicopter of the US Navy, eventually replacing the Kaman Seasprite. This large machine, seen here on a frigate helicopter platform, has now in turn been developed into the SH-60F version for aircraft carriers, with a dunking sonar, MAD, FLIR, ESM and other combat electronic devices, plus Mk 50 torpedoes.*

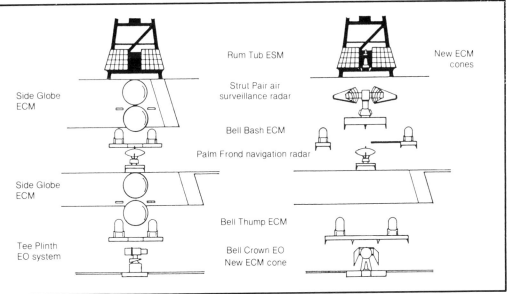

training at airfields but, so far as is known, no proposals have yet been made for a US Navy ship to be constructed with such a fitting.

The unique capabilities of the V/STOL Sea Harrier, combined with the Ski-jump, have led to a wholly new concept in which a suitable merchant-ship could be converted into an aircraft carrier in a matter of days. The Shipborne Con-

tainerised Air-Defence System (SCADS) utilises some 230 standard International Standardisation Organisation (ISO) containers mounted on the deck of a 30,000-ton-plus container ship and topped by a specially prepared flight-deck. The container can be fitted for roles such as missile launcher, fuel storage, aircraft maintenance, personnel accommodation, command post, and so on, to enable a thoroughly

effective aircraft carrier to be produced. This is very similar to the US Navy's Arapaho system, which is currently being tested by the Royal Navy.

British Aerospace have even proposed doing away with a flight-deck altogether; their "Skyhook" design concept is a ship mounted crane which would lift a Sea Harrier outboard and, when the pilot is ready, release it. Recovery requires the aircraft to hover in a notional 10ft (3m) cube area abreast of the crane position and moving forward at the same speed as the ship, whereupon the computer-controlled, space-stabilized crane locks on to the aircraft and lifts it on board. The system envisages all aircraft handling on the ship being done on mechanically operated trestles, which would not only lead to greater efficiency and more economic use of space, but could also much reduce the manpower requirements. Such a system could be mounted in a 5,000-ton hull, which could operate an air squadron of four Sea Harriers and two Sea Kings, thus giving the ship a capability far beyond that previously considered possible for such a small vessel.

An intermediate type flight-deck is used on board some cruiser-sized warships, mainly to enable a large number of helicopters to be operated. Such ships have a conventional superstructure and a large flight-deck aft, and include such types as the Soviet Moskva class (20,000 tons), the Italian *Vittorio Veneto* (8,850 tons) and the French *Jeanne d'Arc* (12,365 tons). Such designs enable normal gun/missile armament to be mounted forward, thus considerably enhancing the ship's ability to look after itself, but the concept is confined to helicopters or VTOL fixed-wing aircraft, and would not be suitable for STOL operations.

## Aircraft on other ships

Finally, virtually every modern cruiser and destroyer, and most frigates now have flight decks and on-board facilities for one, if not two helicopters. This adds immeasurably to their ASW capabilities, since the high speed of modern SSNs in comparison with ship and torpedo speeds means that the helicopter is essential to provide timely response at longer

*Left: One of the tests of the proposed British Aerospace SkyHook. The Harrier Mk 52 demonstrator G-VTOL was used in conjunction with a SkyHook mounted on an ordinary crane to demonstrate the principle in April 1985. Inset drawings show (left) automatic robotics control so that, no matter how the ship may roll and heave in a heavy sea, the SkyHook travels forward in a*

*straight line parallel to the Earth's surface, and (right) a detail of the SkyHook itself showing how the head can swivel or pivot without affecting the orientation of the stabilizing frame located on the aircraft. The original hardware was created with assistance from Dowty, and interest is beginning to harden, for various applications. It could revolutionize the air capabilities of small ships.*

ranges. In addition, a number of modern anti-ship missile systems require an airborne relay/control station to give an Over-the-Horizon (OTH) capability. The smallest hull capable of accommodating a helicopter is the Osprey class of 505 tons, British-designed but built in Denmark, but these are fishery-protection vessels rather than warships, although, obviously, the Osprey design concept could be used for much larger warships. Surprisingly, the new US destroyer design — the Arleigh Burke — will have a flight-deck but no hangar, depending upon other ships in the task group for aircraft maintenance and repair facilities.

Most Western air-capable cruisers and destroyers have large and obvious hangars, whereas the Soviet Navy has developed a very neat (although possibly, mechanically complicated) hangar, which opens up to admit the helicopter and then closes over it. Fitted on ships such as the Kara, Kresta and Udaloy classes, this hangar arrangement has many advantages, although working space for the aircraft engineers may well be very cramped.

Some navies have developed special devices to capture and control helicopters on such small flight decks. Most widely used of these is the Canadian "Bear-trap" device, which is mounted in the centre of the flight deck. Having engaged the trap while hovering some 10ft (3m) above the deck, the helicopter is then hauled down and held firmly on the deck. Other navies, although operating in the same waters as the Canadians, have not considered such a device necessary, proving that helicopters can land on even very small flight decks in almost any sea state.

## The carrier in naval warfare

It is a dangerous over-simplification to regard the aircraft carrier simply as a mobile naval airfield, because it is very much more than that. Apart from the very small carriers, the large fleet carriers are concentrations of air power, command and control facilities, and sensor technology without parallel. The carriers are invariably the largest units in their fleets, let alone in each individual taskforce, and are almost always the flagship. Their very size and the spaciousness of their accommodation enables them to provide the best facilities afloat for commanders and their staffs, with large arrays of communications and sensors. Further, they can carry large and very powerful computer complexes; for example, the American CVNs all house very powerful ASW computers, with real time links not only to the accompanying ships in their task groups, but also, via satellite, back to US and NATO land-based facilities, such as the US Iliad 4.

It is quite clear that the Soviet Union has come to understand this, as is illustrated by the inexorable growth of their carrier capability. This almost certainly stems from the

11

vulnerability they felt in the 1950s and 1960s to American nuclear strike aircraft on board the CVNs of the Forrestal and Kitty Hawk classes, and to which, at that time, they had no real answer. They have also seen how indispensable the carrier is to power projection, since air power is the vital ingredient in any threat to a distant power, or in an amphibious landing. However, even the vast experience and apparently bottomless purse of the Soviet Defence Ministry may find it difficult to produce simultaneously their first 75,000 ton fleet carrier (CVN) and their first carrier-borne fixed-wing attack, fighter, patrol and ASW aircraft.

Mighty as the carrier may appear, and despite all the protection provided by the variety of aircraft in its air wing and its accompanying ASW escorts (both surface and submarine), the aircraft carrier is nevertheless vulnerable. It is quite obviously a high-value target — in terms of naval warfare probably the highest value target of all — and any opponent will therefore inevitably seek to eliminate it at the earliest opportunity.

This was clearly illustrated in the South Atlantic War, where the Argentine carrier, *Vienticinco de Mayo*, was the Royal Navy's primary target, while the Argentines knew that if only they could damage or sink one, if not both, of the British carriers they would compel the Task Force to withdraw to Ascension Island. The British carriers had some very close shaves, and at one point it was only the diversion of an incoming Exocet on to the merchantman the *Atlantic Conveyor* (which it sank) that saved one of the carriers. The American carriers (and the new Soviet ones, too, when they appear) are enormous targets — the Nimitz class are 1,092 ft (317m) long — and while their very size would enable them to absorb a lot of battle damage history suggests that no ship, however sophisticated, is totally invulnerable.

## Weapons

There has been a marked divergence of views on the armament required by aircraft carriers to meet contemporary conditions. In the 1960s the US Navy seemed to go away completely from armament for its aircraft carriers and the Forrestal class ships, for example, which originally had eight 5in guns, had four of these removed in 1967 and the remainder in the early 1970s. Two of the class were then fitted with three Basic Point Defense Missile Systems (BPDMS) each, while the other two now have three. However, following a further reassessment of the threat, especially from sea-skimming missiles, three Phalanx 20mm CIWS are to be fitted during the Service Life Extension Program (SLEP) refits, although this means that USS *Ranger* (CV 61) will not have these weapons until May 1994. Each of the two French aircraft carriers is fitted with eight 3.9in (100mm) automatic guns in

Above: Loading 20mm ammunition, noted for the high-density kinetic-energy penetrator forming the core of each projectile, into a Phalanx CIWS (Close-In Weapon System). Since 1979 General Dynamics, using a pulse-doppler radar and the familiar General Electric M61 gun (controlled to fire at 3,000 rds/min), has sold many hundreds of CIWS installations to navies all over the world. A particular advantage of this installation is that, as it is light and self-contained, it can be simply bolted on a deck almost anywhere, even on a very small ship.

**Task Group protecting merchant convoy:**
In any future war NATO's defence of Europe would depend upon the movement of men, stores and equipment across the Atlantic in vast quantities to reinforce those already "in-place". The Soviet naval and air threat is such that this great move could only take place using the convoy techniques of previous World Wars, but updated wherever possible to take account of the advances in modern technology. The schematic diagram below illustrating how such a task group might be deployed is not to scale, and it must be emphasised that this represents a very large area of sea. Further, although British symbols are used any NATO task group would use similar tactics. The use of many fixed-and rotary-wing aircraft is evident.

| TOTAL RESOURCES AVAILABLE | | | | | |
|---|---|---|---|---|---|
| **Warships** | | **Aircraft** | | **Weapons** | |
| Helicopter Carrier | 1 | Sea Harrier | 5 | Exocet | 36 |
| ASW Frigate | 9 | Sea King | 10 | Sea Dart SAM | 7 |
| AD Frigate | 6 | Lynx | 24 | Sea Wolf SAM | 18 |
| Fleet Oiler | 1 | | | 4.5in Gun | 6 |
| SSN | 3 | | | Sub-Harpoon | Yes |

Fixed-wing, land-based, ASW aircraft eg. P-3 Orion, Nimrod, Atlantique.

Long-range, heavy ASW helicopter, usually carrier-based: eg. Sea King.

Short-range, medium/light ASW helicopter, destroyer/frigate based: eg. Lynx.

Carrier-based fighter aircraft on combat air patrol: eg. Sea Harrier.

Either SSNs or conventional submarines, eg. Valiant class.

High-speed container and passenger ships: convoy 'commodore' commands.

Aircraft carrier, providing air cover and command-and-control facilities.

ASW destroyers/frigates for anti-submarine screen, using own sensors/helicopters.

Inner screen of air defence destroyers/frigates for close air/missile defence.

Naval auxiliaries for Replenishment-at-Sea (RAS) of naval warships.

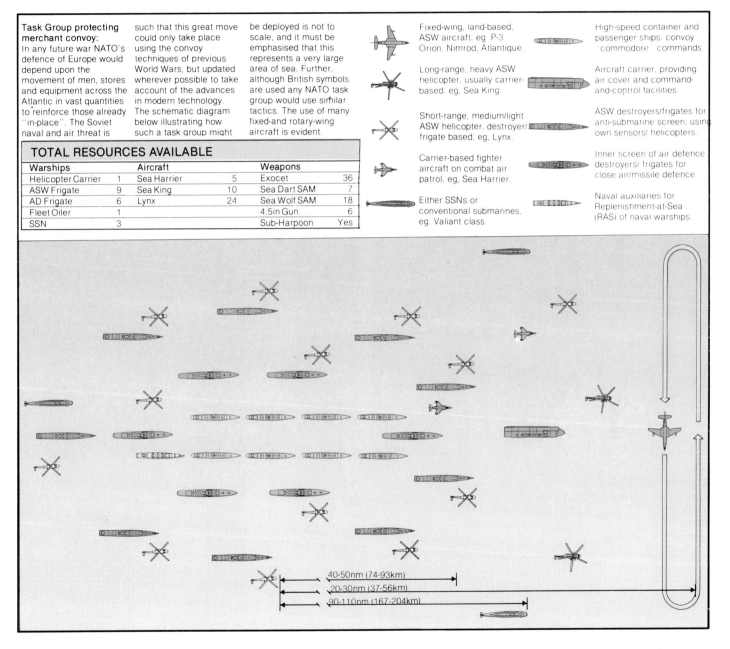

40-50nm (74-93km)
20-30nm (37-56km)
90-110nm (167-204km)

single mounts on sponsons outboard of the flight deck; four will be replaced by Crotale Navale missile systems at their next refits.

A different approach was taken by the Soviet and Italian navies in the 1960s. In this the flight deck was sited in such a way that the foredeck was left clear for a fairly heavy weapons fit. Thus, *Vittorio Veneto* carries one twin SAM launcher, four single Teseo SSM launchers, eight 76mm guns, six twin 40mm guns and two triple torpedo tubes, while the Moskva class vessels have two twin SAM launchers, four 57mm twin guns, one twin SUW-N-1 ASW missile launcher and two 12-barrel RBU-6000 ASW rocket launchers.

Both these navies have, however, modified their design concepts for their respective follow-on classes. The Soviet

Kiev class has an angled deck, though not, as in the Western aircraft carriers, to leave the forward flight deck clear to launch aircraft, but rather to leave the forecastle clear for a heavy weapons fit. In fact, the Kiev's armament is heavier than the total weaponry of a Krivak II frigate. The Italian Navy, on the other hand, needed to fit a ski-jump for the anticipated STOVL aircraft on the *Giuseppe Garibaldi* and therefore adopted a straight-through flight deck; even so, it has still managed to include four Teseo launchers for Otomat SSMs, two Albatros SAM launchers, six 40mm guns and six torpedo tubes.

With the Invincible class light aircraft carriers the Royal Navy fitted a straight-through flight deck, but left the forecastle-head clear for a twin Sea Dart launcher (SAM with a limited SSM capability). Following the 1982 South Atlantic war experience, however, Phalanx 20mm CIWS have been fitted, two in *Invincible* and *Illustrious* and three in *Ark Royal*, while all three now have two 20mm GAM-BO1 single guns installed. The Spanish *Principe de Asturias*, on

the other hand, is armed only with four Meroka 20mm CIWS.

There has been much speculation concerning the armament to be fitted to the Soviet Navy's nuclear powered aircraft carrier *Kremlin*, which was launched in 1985. The various drawings so far released are inevitably highly speculative and disagree on whether the flight deck will continue forward to the bows as in the US Navy's current CVNs and CVs, or will be angled to port, leaving the foredeck clear for armament as on the current Kiev class. There can be little doubt, however, that the Soviet Navy will include the heaviest weapons fit possible on such a large hull

Faced with the high cost of these supercarriers, the concentration of valuable assets in one hull and their unavoidable vulnerability it is frequently suggested that the larger navies, and especially the US Navy, would be better advised to have a numerically greater fleet of much smaller carriers, say in the 30,000 to 40,000 ton range. However, there is no doubt that in the case of the supercarriers large size pays off. First of all, it enables each carrier to embark a

*Far left: An almost head-on view of Novorossiysk, third ship of her class. Hailed by Western media as "the first Soviet carriers", this class in fact introduced a new form of warship which, though unable to deploy conventional fixed-wing airpower, can do everything else. Clearly visible here is her foredeck, saturated with weapons including eight huge tubes for launching "S-N-12 Sandbox" cruise missiles each thought to have a range at Mach 2.5 of 342 miles (550km). The entire port (left) side and rear of the ship is flight deck (here occupied by Ka-27 Helix helicopters), while the mighty superstructure is packed withradars, communications and other electronics.*

*Left: In contrast the far bigger carriers of the US Navy are one-role ships. Their whole design is geared to the operation of their aircraft, and even their own self-defence systems are relatively puny. Their only weapons are for "last ditch" close-in defence against aircraft and missiles, the main weapon being the NSSMS (NATO Sea Sparrow Surface Missile System) seen here being fired from a Mk 29 launcher aboard John F. Kennedy in 1975.*

*Right: This US Government artist's impression (1987) purports to show the giant new Soviet carrier completed fitting out and preparing for sea trials. The flight deck is shown as in US carriers, with one area (with catapults) extending over the bows and another (with catapults) at the front of the angled deck. The name is given as Leonid Brezhnyev, but this is speculative (Kremlin is another suggestion).*

suitably sized air wing with a mix of the various types of aircraft needed to attack the enemy and protect its own task group. (The dreadful problems which faced the British carriers in the South Atlantic War without an AEW aircraft underline this point only too clearly.) Secondly, with CVNs, the compact size of the power plant enables a substantial quantity of aircraft fuel and weaponry to be carried, while the absence of large down- and up-takes leads to a smaller

superstructure, taking up less valuable space on the flight deck. It is for these reasons that the French Navy intends to replace its present CVAs with CVNs towards the end of this decade, with their size being as great as they can afford.

A carrier fleet is thus an essential part of any navy with global pretensions. It will be very interesting to see how the East-West maritime strategic equation alters when the Soviet supercarriers join their fleet.

# 25 de Mayo

Formerly the British light fleet carrier *Venerable,* this vessel was purchased by the Netherlands Navy in 1948 and renamed *Karel Doorman.* She subsequently underwent an extensive modernisation 1955-58, when she was given an angled deck, a single steam catapult forward, and a mirror landing sight. The island was completely rebuilt to accommodate an outfit of Dutch radars, and an armament of 40mm single AA guns was fitted. After modernisation she operated first as an attack carrier, with Sea Hawk fighter-bombers and TBM-3 Avengers, then as an ASW carrier with S-2 Tracker aircraft and HSS-1 (SH-34) Seabat helicopters. In 1965-66 she was reboilered using boilers from the uncompleted British *Leviathan* of the same class.

The ship was badly damaged by a boiler-room fire in 1968, and was subsequently sold to Argentina. She was refitted in the Netherlands before being handed over in 1969, and in the early 1970s a British CAAIS data system compatible with the ADAWS-4 system of the two Type 42 destroyers ordered in 1970 was installed. The air group of the ship during the 1970s comprised A-4 Skyhawks, S-2 Trackers and SH-3 Sea Kings.

In a 1980 refit the flight deck was enlarged abaft the island to permit parking of three additional aircraft, and 14 Super Etendard fighter-bombers were ordered from France to replace the A-4 Skyhawks. Only five of these had been delivered before the Falklands conflict of 1982, and they were operated from land bases. The fact that her catapult was being overhauled in Scotland prevented her participation in the campaign.

**Navy:** Argentina.
**Length:** 698ft (212.7m).
**Beam:** 138ft (42.1m).
**Draught:** 25ft (7.6m).
**Flight deck:** 690x121ft (210.3x37m); angled at 8.5°; one steam catapult.
**Displacement:** 15,892 tons standard; 19,896 full load.
**Propulsion:** 2 shafts; steam turbines, 40,000shp.
**Speed:** 24.25 knots (45km/h).
**Range:** 12,000nm (22,240km) at 14 knots, 6,200 (11,490km) at 23 knots.
**Crew:** 1,005 plus 509 assigned to air group.
**Launched:** 1943.
**Commissioned:** 1945 (UK).
**Air group:** Has embarked up to 10 Super Etendard or 14 A-4Q Skyhawks and 10 S-2 Trackers, and/or S-61A ASW helicopters and Alouette III helicopters for utility and plane guard.
**Armament:** Reconstructed in 1950s with 10 Bofors L90 guns of 40mm calibre, of which nine are currently fitted. In the same refit she was given a comprehensive suite of Dutch radars. Sold to Argentina 1968 and further refitted 1969. Aft flight deck enlarged 1980.

*Below: Laid down in 1942 as a unit in the British Colossus class, this carrier has had an eventful career with three navies, but was spared having to go to war in 1982 by not being able to launch her aircraft. Prior to this conflict consideration had been given to having a major update done in the United Kingdom. Her lattice mast and raked funnel make her look quite different from her original sisters in Australia, India and Brazil.*

*Above right: The venerable Grumman S-2 Tracker remains Argentina's carrier-based fixed-wing ASW aircraft, the force comprising four S-2As and six S-2Es. The Comando de Aviacion Naval has investigated Grumman's Turbo Tracker conversion with TPE331 engines.*

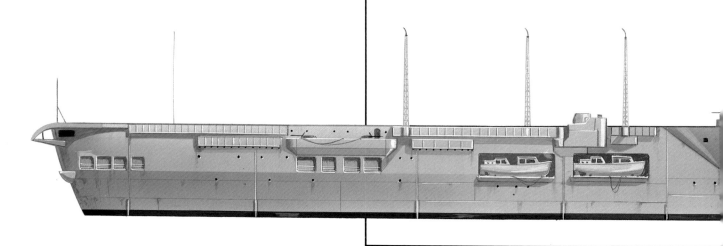

Above: Though the 25 de Mayo languished like this during the "Malvinas war", she is today a considerably more potent ship and can launch the Super Etendard, armed with Exocet missiles.

# Clemenceau

These two light fleet carriers were laid down in the mid1950s and incorporated all the advances in carrier design made in the immediate postwar period. They have served the French Navy well, in both European and Pacific waters, operations in the latter being in support of the remaining French colonial territories and of nuclear tests. They are also among the most powerful units in the Mediterranean and at least one carrier was off Lebanon at all times when French military units were ashore as part of the international peacekeeping forces in Beirut. Following the paying-off of the British aircraft carrier *Ark Royal* these are now the largest units in any European navy.

The Clemenceau class aircraft carriers are fairly conventional in design. The flight deck measures 543ft (165.5m) by 97ft (29.5m) and is angled at 8° to the ship's axis. The forward aircraft lift is offset to starboard with one of the two 170ft (52m) catapults to port; the second catapult is located on the angled deck, and the after lift is positioned on the deck edge to increase hangar capacity. The hangar, which is offset to port, has a usable length of 499ft (152m) and a width of 72-79ft (22-24m), with 23ft (7m) clearance overhead.

A new generation of aircraft was designed to operate from these carriers. Two flights, each of ten Etendard IVM ground support fighters (with integral reconnaissance capability), were initially embarked, together with a flight of Alizé turboprop ASW aircraft, while F-8E Crusaders were purchased from the USA in 1963 and from 1966 made up the interceptor flight. The Etendard IVM has recently been replaced by the Super Etendard, which can carry Exocet anti-ship missiles and has a nuclear strike capability, but the relatively small

Below: In November 1973 the company-owned two-seat Harrier demonstrator G-VTOL made a visit to Foch. Surprisingly, France elected to build a further generation of large (even nuclear propelled) carriers to deploy conventional non-STOVL aircraft.

**Navy:** France.
**Length:** 869.4ft (267m).
**Beam:** 104ft (32m).
**Draught:** 28ft (8.6m).
**Flight deck:** 543x97ft (167x30m); angled at 8°; two catapults.
**Displacement:** 27,307 tons standard; 32,780 full load.
**Propulsion:** 2 geared turbines, 2 shafts, 126,000hp.
**Speed:** 32 knots (59km/h).
**Range:** 7,500nm (13,900km) at 18 knots (33.3km/h).
**Crew:** 1,338.
**Launched:** 1957.
**Commissioned:** 1961.
**Air group:** 40 attack aircraft (mainly Super Etendards); 2 Super Frelon and 2 Alouette III helicopters; Etendard IVP for reconnaissance; 1 Breguet Alizé ASW operations.
**Armament:** Limited to 8 (100mm) automatic guns in single turrets, but of course Super Etendards are capable aircraft, and can carry very effective Exocet anti-ship missiles and other weapons. Air protection seems light.

Above: The eventual armament comprised eight single turrets mounting automatic 100mm guns (3.9in calibre).

Above: A 1981 picture of Clemenceau during an exercise in the Mediterranean. Both vessels have the capability of operating a comprehensive air wing (though about half the size of those of the giant US Navy ships).

Above: The main drawing depicts Clemenceau, though the two units of this class are extremely similar (they do carry pennant numbers on each side of the superstructure, Foch being R99). In general design they resembled the US wartime Essex class, but with modern updates.

size of the ships, together with the limited capacity (20 tonnes) of the lifts and catapults, has made it difficult to find a replacement for the F-8Es. A further limitation on the effectiveness of these ships is their lack of integral airborne early warning (AEW) aircraft, and they would have the same problems as the British Task Force in the 1982 South Atlantic war if they were to deploy against a reasonably sophisticated enemy. Both carriers normally embark two Super Frelon ASW helicopters and two Alouette IIIs.

The French Navy plans to construct two Charles de Gaulle (PAN-1) class nuclear-powered aircraft carriers, the first of which was laid down in 1986 and will join the fleet in 1995. Of 36,000 tons full load displacement, these carriers will have two independent nuclear reactors giving a maximum speed of 27 knots. The weapons fit will include an air defence missile system (three SADRAL fire units with Matra Mistral missiles) and and unspecified anti-missile defence system, and the PAN-1 class will carry a strike group, probably a mix of Super Etendard and a navalized version of the ACT, and their decks will be capable of operating AEW aircraft.

Under present plans *Clemenceau* is due to pay off in 1995, followed by *Foch* in 1998, but this obviously depends upon satisfactory progress with the new nuclear carriers. Meanwhile, both are to be upgraded at their next refits, which will include replacing four 100mm guns by Naval Crotale SAM launchers.

*Above: Clemenceau off the French coast in 1977. These ships have French-built mirror sights but, like most carriers, Scottish-built Mitchell-Brown steam catapults.*

*Below: With the crew "manning ship" Clemenceau during a special review on 11 July 1976. On deck were two Super Frelons and (forward) four Alouette IIIs.*

*Below right: To save money and men the Foch has for many years been basically an ASW ship, operating just Super Frelon helicopters and with a crew of about 984. But the Aéronavale's biggest problem is how to maintain a fighter force between the retirement of the Crusaders and the introduction (around 1977) of the projected Rafale M.*

Weapons
A 100mm dual-purpose
  gun Modèle 1953 (2x1)
B 100mm dual-purpose
  gun Modèle 1953 (2x1)
C 100mm dual-purpose
  gun Modèle 1953 (2x1)
D 100mm dual-purpose
  gun Modèle 1953 (2x1)

Electronics
1 SQS-505 hull-mounted
  sonar
2 DRBC-32A gunfire
  control radar
3 DRBN-32 navigation
  radar (Decca 1226)
4 DRBI-10C height-
  finding radar

5 DRBV-23B air surveil-
  lance radar
6 DRBV-50 surface
  search radar
7 SRN-6 Tacan antenna
8 DRBV-20C long-range
  search radar
9 DRBI-10C height-
  finding radar
10 Carrier Control
   Approach (CCA) radar

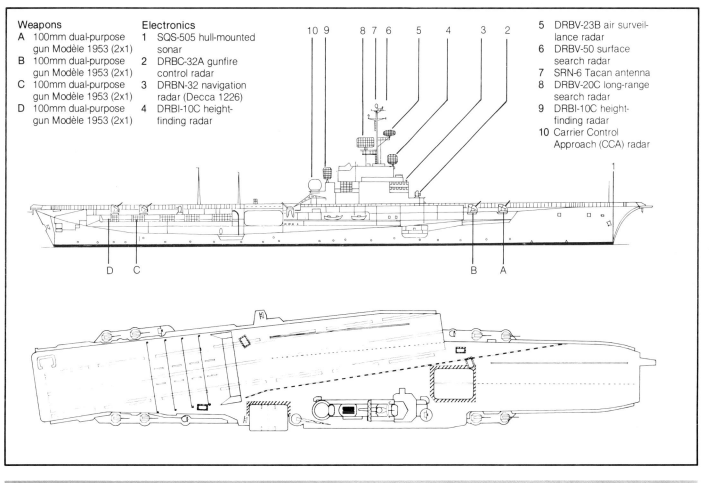

# Dédalo

In 1967 the former US Navy aviation transport *Cabot*, refitted as an ASW helicopter carrier, was transferred to Spain for a period of five years. She was purchased outright in 1973, and since 1976 has operated AV-8S Harrier V/STOL aircraft (re-christened "Matador" in Spanish service) in addition to her antisubmarine helicopters. *Dédalo* is currently flagship of the Spanish fleet; she will be replaced by the new purpose-built *Príncipe de Asturias*.

**Navy:** Spain.
**Completed:** 1943.
**Names:** R01 Dédalo.
**Displacement:** 13,000 tons standard; 16,416 tons full load.
**Dimensions:** Length overall 622ft 6in (189.7m); beam 109ft 2 in (33.3m); draught 26ft 7in (8.1m).
**Elevators:** 2 centre-line, 44ft x 42ft (13.4m x 12.8m).
**Catapults:** None.
**Propulsion:** 4-shaft geared steam turbines; 100,000shp = 31kt.
**Armament:** 22 40mm (1 x 4, 9 x 2).
**Aircraft:** 5AV-8S Matador; SH-3D Sea King; 4 AB 212ASW.
**Complement:** 1,100 ( + air group).

*Below: Built as a second-line ship in World War II, with a wooden deck, the* Dédalo *has put up a flawless performance as a base for the AV-8A Matador (Harrier I). There are many in the Spanish Navy who hope she will be allowed to stay in commission into the 1990s.*

# Enterprise

Laid down shortly after the US Navy's first nuclear-powered surface ship, the cruiser *Long Beach*, *Enterprise* was completed in the remarkably short space of 3 years 9 months. In order to provide sufficient power for a top speed of 30kt no less than eight nuclear reactors had to be accommodated, and the entire centre section of the ship below hangar deck level is taken up by machinery. *Enterprise* cost nearly twice as much to build as her fossil-fuelled contemporaries of the Kitty Hawk class but a number of strong arguments were advanced in favour of nuclear power: the nuclear powered carrier would have reduced life-cycle costs due to infrequent refuellings, and would be capable of lengthy transits and continuous operations in high-threat areas at a high sustained speed. Moreover, the elimination of ship's fuel bunkers in *Enterprise* allowed a 50 per cent increase in aviation fuel capacity, and consequently in the number of consecutive days of strike operations she could sustain.

In size and general layout *Enterprise* is similar to the Kitty Hawk class. The most significant difference as completed was in the configuration of the island, a "box" structure on which "billboard" planar radar arrays were mounted. In a major refit 1979-81 this was replaced by a more conventional structure with rotating radars. *Enterprise* was to have received two Mk 10 launchers for Terrier missiles, but these were never installed and she is now fitted with NATO Sea Sparrow launchers and Phalanx CIWS guns. Since the mid-1960s *Enterprise* has operated with the Pacific Fleet.

In December 1987 she was undergoing maintenance at Alameda (San Francisco Bay), but three months later was unexpectedly in action in the troubled Gulf area protecting international shipping, as a unit of the Atlantic Fleet.

*Right: Looking down on CVN-65, the US Navy's first nuclear-powered carrier. She has now been rebuilt with a super-structure more akin to that of the Nimitz class.*

*Right:* Dédalo with helicopters (including SH-3Ds) in condition of immediate readiness. Whether or not the AV-8A Matador remains operational, this ship is likely to remain in commission into the next decade.

*Left: An air traffic controller aboard CVN-65 taking the vital human decisions which could, in a crisis situation, mean life or death to air traffic. Aided by E-2C Hawkeyes, the controllers aboard US Navy supercarriers can command and control all air traffic within a 250 mile (400km) radius.*

**Navy:** United States.
**Length:** 1,123ft (342.3m).
**Beam:** 248ft (75.6m).
**Draught:** 36ft (11m).
**Flight deck:** 1,100x252ft (335x76.8m); angled at 8°; 4 steam catapults.
**Displacement:** 75,700 tons standard; 89,600 full load.
**Propulsion:** 4 shafts; steam turbines, nuclear boiler heat, 280,000shp.
**Speed:** 33 knots (61km/h).
**Range:** About 13 years, roughly 1 million miles.
**Crew:** 3,100 plus 2,400 assigned to air wing.
**Launched:** 1960.
**Commissioned:** 1961.
**Air wing:** 24 F-14A/D Tomcat, 24 F/A-18A Hornet, 10 A-6E Intruder, 10 S-3A/B Viking and 6SH-3H Sea King; in support, 4 E-2C Hawkeye, 4 KA-6D tanker.
**Armament:** 2 BPDMS (Basic Point Defence Missile System) of Mk 29 type, each with box housing 8 NATO Sea Sparrow missiles; three Mk 15 Phalanx 20mm CIWS.

Above: Bow-on view of this famous carrier prior to reconstruction of her superstructure. Today she is much closer in most respects to the later Nimitz class, the current standard.

Left: CVN-65 Enterprise engaged in exercise CINCPAC Fleetex '83, in 1983. Shortly after this she went in for a major refit and upgrade.

# Forrestal

The overall size and the aircraft-handling arrangements of the Forrestal class were dictated by the requirement to operate the A-3 Skywarrior strategic bomber, which weighed fully 78,000lb (35,380kg). Hangar height was increased from 17ft 6in (5.3m) in the Midway class to 25ft (7.6m), and aviation fuel capacity from 365,000 gallons to 750,000 gallons. The original design was for a carrier similar in configuration to the ill-fated *United States,* which had a flush deck, together with a retractable bridge, and two waist catapults angled out on sponsons in addition to the customary pair of catapults forward. The advent of the angled deck, which was tested by the US Navy in 1952 on the Essex-class carrier *Antietam,* led to the modification of *Forrestal* while building to incorporate this new development. The result was the distinctive configuration which has been adopted by all subsequent US carrier construction: a massive flight deck with considerable overhang, and a small island incorporating the smokestack to starboard. Deck-edge lifts were incorporated in the overhang, resulting in a large uninterrupted hangar in which more than half the ship's aircraft could be accommodated. As completed the Forrestal class was armed with eight 5in (127mm) single gun mountings, but these were steadily removed and by the late 1970s had been replaced by BPDMS and NATO Sea Sparrow missile launchers.

Unlike later carriers the Forrestal class ships do not operate the F-14 Tomcat but retain the F-4 Phantom. *Ranger* serves in the Pacific, and the other three in the Atlantic. *Saratoga* was taken in hand in October 1980 for a three-year major modernisation (Service Life Extension Program, SLEP) which will enable her to remain operational into the 1990s. The other three ships will follow.

**Navy:** United States.
**Length:** 1,086ft (331m).
**Beam:** (hull) 129.5ft (39.5m).
**Draught:** 37ft (11.3m).
**Flight deck:** 1,000x252ft (305x76.8m); angled at 8°; 4 steam catapults.
**Displacement:** 59,060 tons standard; 75,900 full load.
**Propulsion:** 4 shafts; steam turbines, 260,000shp.
**Speed:** 33 knots (61km/h).
**Range:** 6,625nm (12,875km) at 20 knots.
**Crew:** 2,790 plus about 2,150 assigned to air wing.
**Launched:** 1954.
**Commissioned:** 1955.
**Air wing:** 12 F-14A/D Tomcat, 24 F/A-18A Hornet, 10 A-6E Intruder, 10 S-3A/B Viking and 6 SH-3H Sea King; in support, 4 E-2C Hawkeye, 4 KA-6D tanker.
**Armament:** 2 BPDMS (Basic Point Defence Missile System) of Mk 29 type, each with box housing 8 NATO Sea Sparrow missiles.

The lead ship, Forrestal; her sisters are very similar. The elevator at the front of the angled deck was inconvenient.

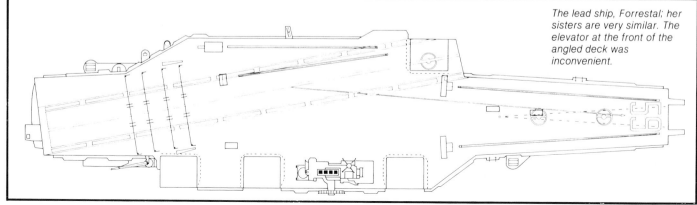

Left: An A-7E is launched from Saratoga in the Med in January 1986. The bows of all US carriers are broadly alike.

Below: Bow-on aspect of CV-60 Saratoga operating in the Mediterranean in April 1984, after her SLEP modernisation.

Above: A-7Es, A-6Es, F-14As and a single S-3A can be seen ranged on Saratoga's deck during operations off Libya in February 1986.

Below: Another view of Saratoga, second of the class. The third and fourth units, respectively, were Ranger and Independence.

# Giuseppe Garibaldi

*Giuseppe Garibaldi* is the first purpose-built, through-deck carrier to be completed for the Italian Navy. She is designed primarily for anti-submarine warfare, operating the big SH-3D Sea King in place of the AB204/212 helicopters embarked by the previous generation of Italian ASW cruisers. She is also intended to be able to counter threats from aircraft and surface ships, and can mount amphibious operations as well as taking part in disaster relief operations.

The hangar is located centrally and is 361ft (110m) long and 20ft (6m) high, with a maximum width of 49ft (15m). The centre section, however, is somewhat narrower due to the gas-turbine uptakes to starboard. The hangar is divided into three sections by fire curtains and can accommodate either 12 Sea Kings or a slightly smaller number of the new EH.101 helicopters, or 10 Sea Harriers. Two hexagonal lifts are off-set to starboard fore and aft of the massive island, each measuring 59ft (18m) by 33ft (10m) and with a capacity of 15 tons. The flight deck has a 6° ski-jump for V/STOL aircraft and is marked with six helicopter spots.

The principal ASW weapon system is the SH-3D Sea King helicopter, which also has a surface warfare role providing mid-course guidance for the ship-launched Otomat Mk 2 (Teseo) anti-ship missiles. There are two double Teseo launchers fitted on each quarter, plus an octuple launcher on each end of the island superstructure for the Selenia Albatros point defence system, which fires Aspide missiles. Close-in defence is provided by the Selenia Elsag Dardo system, using three twin Breda 40mm gun mounts, one on each bow and the third amidships aft.

Above: Italy's sole platform for seagoing combat aircraft is seen here on the slipway at the Italcantieri yard at Monfalcone, which previously was famed for submarines.

**Navy:** Italy.
**Length:** 591ft (180.2m).
**Beam:** 76.8ft (23.4m).
**Draught:** 22ft (6.7m).
**Flight deck:** 565x98ft (174x30.4m); no catapults; 6.5° ski-jump.
**Displacement:** 10,100 tons standard; 13,320 full load.
**Propulsion:** 2 shafts, 4 gas turbines, 80,000hp.
**Speed:** 30 knots (55.5km/h).
**Range:** 7,000nm (12,970km) at 20 knots (37km/h).
**Crew:** 550 plus 230 air group.
**Launched:** 1983.
**Commissioned:** 1985.
**Air group:** Accommodation for: 12 SH-3D helicopters in hangar, plus 4 on deck; or 10 Sea Harriers plus 1 SH-3D in hangar. (EH101 helicopters to replace SH-3DS.)
**Armament:** 3 sets of twin-mount, 40/70 cannon plus Albatros launch rails and Aspide missiles for anti-aircraft and anti-missile; 4 double launch rails for Otomat Mk.2 anti-ship missiles; triple torpedo tubes.

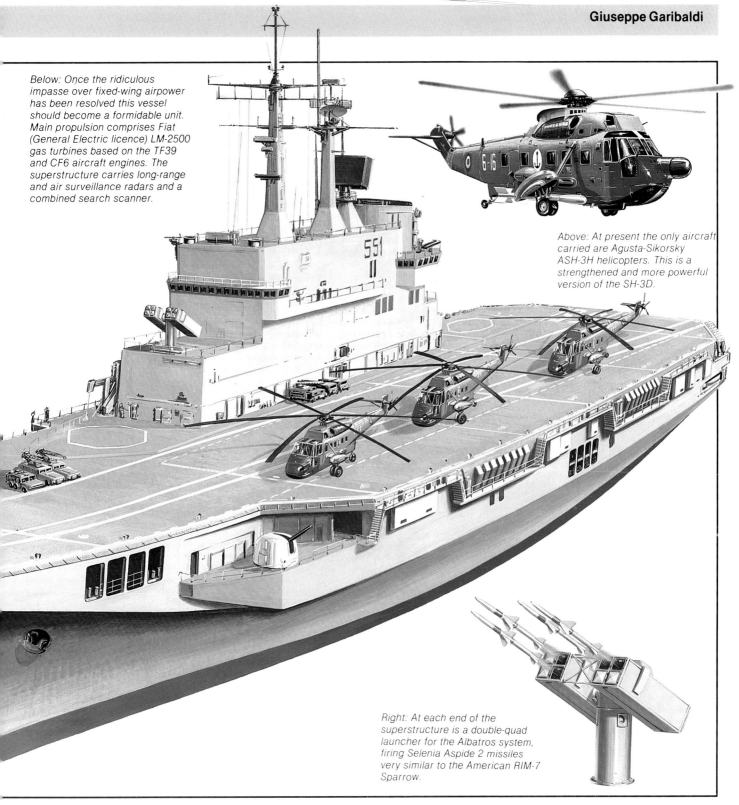

Below: Once the ridiculous impasse over fixed-wing airpower has been resolved this vessel should become a formidable unit. Main propulsion comprises Fiat (General Electric licence) LM-2500 gas turbines based on the TF39 and CF6 aircraft engines. The superstructure carries long-range and air surveillance radars and a combined search scanner.

Above: At present the only aircraft carried are Agusta-Sikorsky ASH-3H helicopters. This is a strengthened and more powerful version of the SH-3D.

Right: At each end of the superstructure is a double-quad launcher for the Albatros system, firing Selenia Aspide 2 missiles very similar to the American RIM-7 Sparrow.

Instead of having reversing controllable-pitch propellers the *Garibaldi* is fitted with a Franco-Tosi reversing hydraulic coupling, which enables fixed-pitch propellers to be used, for maximum propulsive efficiency and minimum noise. Each propeller has five blades and a maximum speed of 175 rpm.

*Giuseppe Garibaldi* has been at the centre of a major political row in Italy as the ship is clearly designed to operate V/STOL aircraft such as the Sea Harrier — the ski-jump forward can have no other purpose. However, under a law dating back to 1923 the Navy is not permitted to operate fixed-wing aircraft and the Italian Air Force has steadfastly refused to procure and operate such types for the Navy. Nevertheless, *Garibaldi* is now at sea as the flagship of the fleet and senior Italian naval officers are still campaigning for authority to operate fixed-wing aircraft.

There are only two aircraft which could fulfil the require-ment: the British Aerospace Sea Harrier FRS.2 and the McDonnell Douglas AV-B Harrier II. Even if a purchase is finally approved, however, it will take some further time for the Italian Navy to work up a fixed-wing component, a field in which they have no previous experience, and presumably technical assistance would be included in any purchase deal.

Even without its fixed-wing aircraft this is a formidable ship, which considerably enhances the NATO fleet capability in the Mediterranean. Somewhat smaller and cheaper than the British Invincible class, it makes an interesting comparison with the Spanish *Principe de Asturias*.

This ship is intended to replace the ageing *Andrea Doria* and *Caio Duilio*. It was very expensive and its fixed wing component (Harrier II/Sea Harrier), if bought, will add considerably to the cost. It is unlikely, therefore, that any more units of this class will be built.

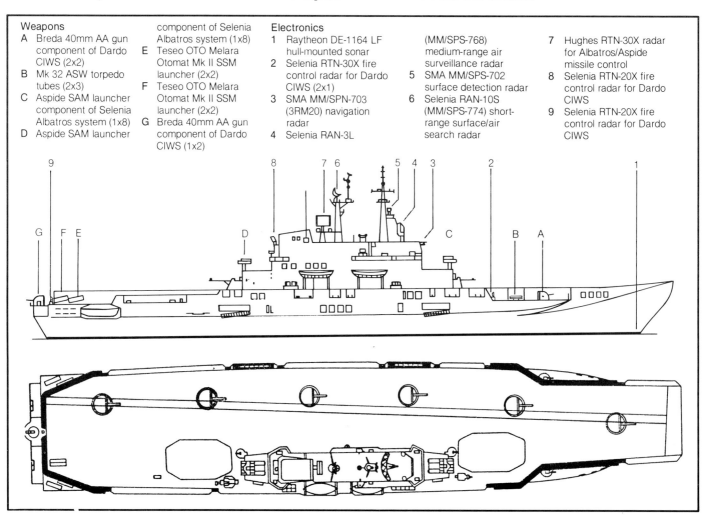

**Weapons**
A  Breda 40mm AA gun component of Dardo CIWS (2x2)
B  Mk 32 ASW torpedo tubes (2x3)
C  Aspide SAM launcher component of Selenia Albatros system (1x8)
D  Aspide SAM launcher component of Selenia Albatros system (1x8)
E  Teseo OTO Melara Otomat Mk II SSM launcher (2x2)
F  Teseo OTO Melara Otomat Mk II SSM launcher (2x2)
G  Breda 40mm AA gun component of Dardo CIWS (1x2)

**Electronics**
1  Raytheon DE-1164 LF hull-mounted sonar
2  Selenia RTN-30X fire control radar for Dardo CIWS (2x1)
3  SMA MM/SPN-703 (3RM20) navigation radar
4  Selenia RAN-3L (MM/SPS-768) medium-range air surveillance radar
5  SMA MM/SPS-702 surface detection radar
6  Selenia RAN-10S (MM/SPS-774) short-range surface/air search radar
7  Hughes RTN-30X radar for Albatros/Aspide missile control
8  Selenia RTN-20X fire control radar for Dardo CIWS
9  Selenia RTN-20X fire control radar for Dardo CIWS

*Above: The scene at Monfalcone on the day of the launch in 1981.*

*After the launch the ship was armed and equipped.*

*Below: In most essentials the Italian carrier is a "through-deck cruiser" though smaller and with far more weapons.*

# Invincible

Following the mid-1960s political decision not to proceed with a new generation of attack carriers for the Royal Navy, design work started on a large, air-capable anti-submarine cruiser for deployment within the NATO EASTLANT area of operations. The design went through a series of changes in response to both political and naval manoeuvring in the British Ministry of Defence.

Originally intended to operate only large helicopters, this vessel was subject to late design changes to enable it to operate the Sea Harrier STOVL aircraft needed to intercept hostile reconnaissance and ASW aircraft, while a final change in 1976-77 established a requirement for the type to be capable of operating as commando cruisers. The original designation of 'through-deck cruiser' (adopted primarily for political reasons) was dropped in 1980 and the type was given the more accurate designation of ASW carrier.

Unlike previous Royal Navy carriers, but following the lead given, for example, by the Italian *Vittorio Veneto* and the Soviet *Moskva*, the Invincible class has an open forecastle-head deck which is utilized for weapons systems. The current fit comprises a twin Sea Dart GWS.30 SAM launcher with a 22-round magazine, supplemented as a result of the lessons of the 1982 South Atlantic war by Phalanx 20mm CIWS. In *Invincible* and *Illustrious* the first Phalanx is mounted on the forecastle alongside the Sea Dart launcher and the second is mounted at the after end of the flight deck on the starboard side.

*Ark Royal*, the last of the three to be completed, has three Phalanx: the first is mounted in the eyes of the ship, the second at the forward end of the flight-deck on the starboard

Above: Invincible on trials from the builders, Vickers of Barrow, with Ailsa Craig rock in the background. Her sisters were both built by Swan Hunter at Wallsend.

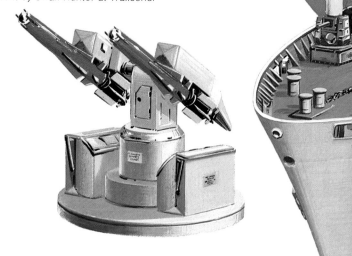

Above: Amazingly, the sole armament of these large ships was a twin launcher for Sea Dart SAMs. Reloads come up vertically through the large boxes on each side.

**Navy:** United Kingdom.
**Length:** 671ft (206.6m).
**Beam:** 90ft (27.5m).
**Draught:** 24ft (7.4m).
**Flight deck:** 545ft (167.8m) length; ski-jump varies from 7° to 15° with ship; no catapults.
**Displacement:** 16,000 tons standard; 19,500 full load.
**Propulsion:** 4 gas turbines; 2 shafts; 112,000shp.
**Speed:** 28 knots (52km/h).
**Range:** 5,000nm (9,265km) at 18 knots (33.3km/h).
**Crew:** 1,000 ship, plus air group.
**Launched:** 1977.
**Commissioned:** 1980.
**Air group:** *Invincible:* up to 10 Sea Harriers plus nine Sea King helicopters. *Illustrious:* two extra Sea King AEW helicopters (to be 3 on all ships eventually).
**Armament:** Two 20mm Phalanx CIWS; 529 20mm cannon, plus Sea Dart missile installation, for anti-aircraft and anti-missile operation. (Sea Dart may also be used as an anti-ship weapon).

Below: The main drawing depicts Illustrious, which was finally completed with the Sea Dart launcher in the original location and only a 7° (instead of the planned 15°) ski-jump. The two giant "funnels" are casings surrounding the exhaust uptakes from the four Rolls-Royce Olympus gas turbines. Including aircrew the complement is about 950.

Below: Invincible pictured during exercises in November 1985. Her Sea Dart missiles are bright red, and flight-deck support equipment yellow. Sea Kings were HAS.2s.

side and the third on a sponson on the port quarter just below flight-deck level. *Ark Royal* also has two twin BMARC 30mm mountings: one on a flight-deck level sponson on the starboard side abreast the mainmast, and the second on a larger sponson on the port side at hangar deck level. The Sea Dart, apart from being a highly effective SAM, also has a very reasonable anti-ship capability.

The flight-deck, which measures 550ft (167.8m) in length and 44ft (13.4m) in width, is very slightly angled and is offset to port to clear the Sea Dart launcher. The ski-jump at the forward end of the flight-deck is angled at 7° on *Invincible* and *Illustrious* and 12° on *Ark Royal*. Underneath this flight-deck is the aircraft hangar, which narrows somewhat at the centre due to the exhaust uptakers for the gas turbines on the starboard side. This is not too serious for helicopter handling but does impose some constraints for the Sea Harriers.

The usual peacetime aircraft complement is 14, normally divided into nine Sea Kings and five Sea Harriers (eight from 1988). As a result of experience in the South Atlantic two of the Sea Kings will almost invariably be of the AEW version. Furthermore, in wartime the number of aircraft can be increased by using deck parks, allowing up to 10 Sea Harriers to be embarked.

As these ships will obviously be used to command ASW task groups they are fitted with a very comprehensive command centre, which has proved its worth on many NATO exercises. That on *Invincible* also proved invaluable during Operation Corporate, the British undertaking to repossess the Falkland Islands. Prior to that operation the British Government planned to offer *Invincible* for sale to the Royal Australian Navy, but the value of this class was made so clear that the plan was quickly shelved at the war's end.

*Ark Royal*, in addition to the armament differences noted

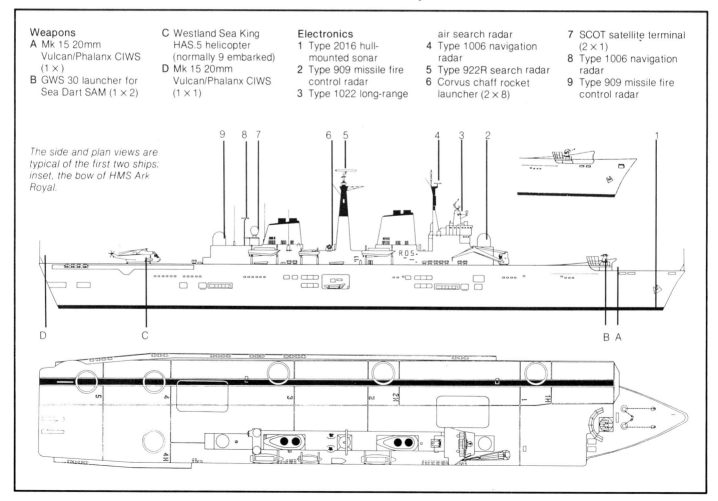

Weapons
A Mk 15 20mm Vulcan/Phalanx CIWS (1 ×)
B GWS 30 launcher for Sea Dart SAM (1 × 2)
C Westland Sea King HAS.5 helicopter (normally 9 embarked)
D Mk 15 20mm Vulcan/Phalanx CIWS (1 × 1)

Electronics
1 Type 2016 hull-mounted sonar
2 Type 909 missile fire control radar
3 Type 1022 long-range air search radar
4 Type 1006 navigation radar
5 Type 922R search radar
6 Corvus chaff rocket launcher (2 × 8)
7 SCOT satellite terminal (2 × 1)
8 Type 1006 navigation radar
9 Type 909 missile fire control radar

*The side and plan views are typical of the first two ships: inset, the bow of HMS Ark Royal.*

above, has other changes from the first two of the class. The ship's interior has been redesigned with better workshop space, more storerooms and better living accommodation. The hangar is fitted out to take the Anglo-Italian EH.101 helicopter when that machine enters service in the 1990s, and greatly improved electronic systems are also fitted.

The design, size and capabilities of the Invincible class make a very interesting comparison with the Italian *Giuseppe Garibaldi* and the Spanish *Principe de Asturias*.

These ships have already served the Royal Navy well, and, in view of what happened in the 1982 South Atlantic war, it is as well that the *Invincible* was available for the Task Force. The additional features in *Ark Royal* amount to those destined for her two pre-decessors at their first refit. There has been no discussion on the next generation of aircraft carrier for the Royal Navy, which may well cause a crisis as severe as that over CVA-01, purely on the grounds of cost.

*Above: Illustrious differs from her predecessor only in detail.*

*Above right: Ark Royal before she was fitted with augmented close-range air defence armament (three CIWS Phalanx and two twin single-barrel 30mm guns, one on each side). She has a 12° ski jump; originally it had been planned to fit the second and third ships with a 15° ramp. In 1988 Ark was first to embark a Sea Harrier squadron with eight aircraft instead of the previous five.*

*Right: A 1983 picture of Invincible, when her CIWS had just been fitted. The original design of these ships also provided for four launchers for Exocet missiles but these were never fitted.*

# Kiev

Classified by the Soviet Navy as *takticheskye avianostny kreysera* (tactical aircraft-carrying cruisers), the four ships of the Kiev class incorporate the lessons learned from the Moskva class but are equipped with an angled flight-deck to enable them to operate V/STOL aircraft as well as helicopters. As with the Moskvas, however, the forward part of the ship has been devoted to gun and missile systems, giving the Kievs a unique carrier/cruiser configuration. These are very impressive ships which, in addition to their wartime tasks, have obvious applications in projecting Soviet seapower on a global scale during peacetime deployments.

The basic concepts of the Kiev class design originated in the 1960s when the main threat to the Soviet Union was

**Navy:** Soviet Union.
**Length:** 899ft (274m).
**Beam:** 158ft (48m).
**Draught:** 33ft (10m).
**Flight deck:** 620x68ft (189x20.7m) 4.5° angle; no catapults.
**Displacement:** 33,500 tons standard; 38,000 full load.
**Propulsion:** 4-shaft; geared turbines, 180,000hp.
**Speed:** 32 knots (59km/h).
**Range:** 13,500nm (25,000km) at 18 knots (33km/h).
**Crew:** 1,200 ship, plus air group.
**Launched:** 1972.
**Commissioned:** 1975.
**Air group:** 12 Yak-38 ''Forger'' V/STOL attack (2-seat trainers also carried); 14 Ka-27 ''Helix-A'' helicopters for ASW; 6 Ka-25 ''Hormone-B'' for missile guidance; Ka-27 ''Helix-D'' for plane-guard duty.
**Armament:** 8 S-N-12 SSM launchers; 2 twin SA-N-3, 2 twin SA-N-4 launchers; 2 twin 76.2mm DP guns; 8 30mm Gatling CIWS; 1 twin SUW-N-1 ASW launcher; 2 RBU-6000 launchers; 2x5 21in (533mm) torpedo tubes.

*Facing page: A fine picture of the third unit of this important class, Novorossiysk. The first three ships are generally similar, but fortunately (since pennant numbers often change) all carry their name in giant metal characters on the bows and transom.*

*Facing page inset: Stern view of the first ship of the class, giving an indication of the large volume available in the big and extraordinarily versatile ships. Yak-38s are on deck.*

*Left: The main drawing is, of course, the lead ship of the class, Kiev. Her amazing array of weapons is clearly depicted, each element being identified with the drawing on overleaf.*

*Right: One of the most impressive features of Soviet surface warships — in sharpest contrast to the Royal Navy in the Falklands — is their multiple 30mm "Gatling" AA armament.*

assessed to be the US Navy's Polaris submarines (SSBNs). The Kievs' primary mission is, therefore, ASW and the ships carry an outfit of weapon systems almost identical to that of the Moskva class: a squadron of some 16 Ka-25 Hormone-A helicopters, an SUW-N-1 launcher for FRAS-1 missiles, two anti-submarine rocket launchers and two quintuple banks of torpedo tubes. Target data is provided by a large low-frequency bow sonar and a stern-mounted variable-depth sonar, supplemented, of course, by data from the ship's ASW helicopters and other ships in the task unit.

The air defence missile systems are more extensive than in the Moskvas and are split between the forecastle and the after end of the island superstructure to give a good all-round coverage. A particularly heavy CIWS armament is fitted, consisting of eight of the Soviet Navy's standard 30mm Gatlings, and an impressive anti-ship capability is provided by the four pairs of SS-N-13 launchers located on the forecastle, with a reload magazine between them.

The flight-deck is angled at 4.5° and is marked with seven helicopter spots and a large circle aft for Yakolev Yak-38 Forger landings. The angled portion of the flight deck and the after deck aircraft park are covered with heat-resistant tiles to absorb the heat from the Forger's two vertical lift engines. A long hangar runs beneath the flight-deck; the forward section is probably some 49ft (15m) wide increasing to about 69ft (21m) aft and up to 35 aircraft can be accommodated. There are two aircraft lifts; the larger is amidships, between the angled eck and the island superstructure, while the other is immediately aft of the island. There are several smaller lifts for deck tractors, personnel and munitions.

All four ships of this class (*Kiev, Minsk, Novorossiysk* and *Baku*) are now in service, giving the Soviet Navy an un-precedented blue ocean capability. In April 1985, for example, a carrier battle group consisting of *Novorossiysk*, three Kara I and one Kresta II cruisers, and one Krivak I and one Krivak II frigates deployed from Vladivostok into the Pacific Ocean. Leaving the frigates, the larger ships moved initially at a speed of 14-18 knots, but the return to the Tsushima Straits was carried out at a speed of 20 knots, a very high cruising speed. This was a very successful and impressive operation, although the carrier group far outstripped its replenishment tankers, which would lead to severe logistic problems in wartime.

The first of the class, *Kiev*, has recently finished her first major refit; this lasted two years, but full details of the changes have not yet been published. She has been seen, however, operating her Forger-A aircraft in rolling take-offs, a capability previously demonstrated only by *Novorossiysk*; these takeoffs are being performed on the standard deck and not, as at one time predicted, from a ski-jump.

It would appear that the Soviet Navy will keep these four ships in service for many years, updating them as necessary in their periodic refits. Construction appears to have ended with the fourth ship, *Baku*, and all efforts are now being concentrated on the new Kremlin class nuclear powered carriers, the first of which was laid down in 1983 and launched in December 1985 at the Nikolayev yard on the Black sea; she was due to start sea trials in 1988.

*Below left: Minsk, the second of the class, under way in northern waters. The Ka-25 helicopters have now been replaced by Ka-27s, but a successor to the Yak-38 has not yet been seen.*

*Below: The foredeck of Minsk, showing what must be the most impressive fit of modern weapon systems of any warship in the world. By comparison other carriers are almost defenceless!*

## Weapons

A  RBU-6000 ASW rocket launcher (1 × 16)
B  RBU-6000 ASW rocket launcher (1 × 16)
C  SUW-N-1 ASW missile launcher (1 × 2)
D  76mm dual-purpose gun mounting (1 × 2)
E  SS-N-12 launcher (2 × 2)
F  SA-N-3 launcher (1 × 2)
G  SS-N-12 launcher (2 × 2)
H  21in (533mm) torpedo tubes (2 × 5)
J  SA-N-4 pop-up launcher (1 × 2)
K  ADMG-630 30mm Gatling CIWS (2 × 1)
L  ADMG-630 30mm Gatling CIWS (1 × 2)
M  SA-N-3 launcher (1 × 2)
N  76mm dual-purpose gun mounting (2 × 2)
O  SA-N-4 pop-up launcher (1 × 2)
P  Kamov Ka-25 Hormone or Ka-27 Helix ASW helicopters (16A plus 3B)
Q  Yakovlev Yak-38 Forger (12A plus 1B)
R  ADMG-630 30mm Gatling CIWS (2 × 1)
S  ADMG-630 30mm Gatling CIWS (1 × 2)

## Electronics

1  Trap Door missile control radar for SS-N-12
2  LF hull-mounted sonar
3  Chaff launcher (2 × 1)
4  Bass Tilt fire control radar for CIWS
5  Owl Screech fire control radar for 76mm gun
6  Don-Kay navigation radar
7  Punch Bowl satellite navigation system (2 × 1) (Pop Group on opposite side of superstructure)
8  Headlight missile
9  Tee Plinth optronic device (2 × 1)
10 Don 2 navigation radar (2 × 1)
11 Top Sail 3D air surveillance radar
12 Vee-Bars HF antenna system (2 × 1)
13 High Pole IFF antenna
14 Top Knot aircraft navigation system
15 Rum Tub ESM antenna arrays (2 × 2)
16 Top Steer surveillance radar
17 Side Globe EW antennas (2 × 4)
control radar SA-N-3
18 Pop Group missile control radar for SA-N-4 (Punch Bowl on opposite side of superstructure
19 Headlight Missile control radar for SA-N-3
20 Owl Screech fire control radar for 76mm gun
21 Chaff launcher (2 × 1)
22 Bass Tilt fire control radar for CIWS
23 MF variable depth sonar

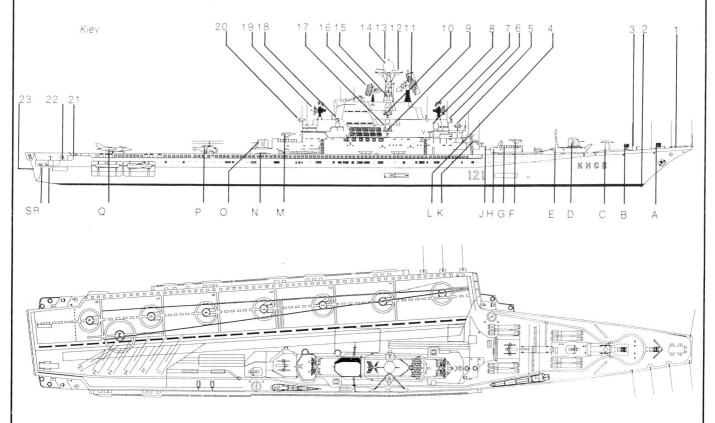

*Kiev*

This drawing shows a typical arrangement for the first three ships. The fourth, Baku, has a completely different super-structure, with a huge group of phased-array radars, a gigantic 360° (radar?) drum on top, two twin 76mm gun turrets and one row of eight SS-N-12 tubes.

# Kitty Hawk

There are major differences between the first pair of air-craft carriers completed, *Kitty Hawk* (CV 63) and *Constellation* (CV 64), and the second two, *America* (CV 66) and *John F Kennedy* (CV 66). These four ships are, however, generally grouped together because of their common propulsions systems and flight-deck layout.

*Kitty Hawk* and *Constellation* were ordered as improved versions of the Forrestal class, incorporating a number of important modifications. The flight-deck was increased slightly in area, and the layout of the lifts revised to enhance aircraft-handling arrangements. On the Forrestals the port side lift is located at the forward end of the angled deck, making it unusable during landing operations, so the lift was repositioned at the after end of the overhang on the Kitty Hawks, where it no longer interferes with flying operations. In addition, the centre lift on the starboard side has been repositioned to be ahead of the island structure, enabling two lifts to be used to serve the forward catapults.

A further improved feature of the lifts themselves is that an angled section at the forward end enables longer aircraft to be accommodated. This arrangement is so successful that it has been copied in all subsequent US carriers.

The third ship of the class, *America* (CV 66), was laid down four years after *Constellation* and incorporates a number of further modifications. She has a narrower smokestack and is fitted with a bow anchor, in anticipation of the fitting of an SQS-23 sonar. It was decided in 1963 that the fourth carrier due to be laid down in FY1984 should be nuclear powered, but Congress flatly refused to fund it and the ship was finally built to a modifided Kitty Hawk design as a conventionally powered carrier.

**Navy:** United States.
**Length:** 1,046ft (318.8m).
**Beam:** (hull) 130ft (39.6m).
**Draught:** 37ft (11.3m).
**Flight deck:** 1,000x252ft (305x76.8m); angled at 8°; 4 steam catapults.
**Displacement:** 60,100 tons standard; 80,800 full load.
**Propulsion:** 4 shafts; steam turbines, 280,000shp.
**Speed:** 33 knots (61km/h).
**Range:** 7,700nm (12,970km).
**Crew:** 2,800 plus about 2,150 assigned to air wing.
**Launched:** 1960.
**Commissioned:** 1961.
**Air wing:** 24 F-14A/D Tomcat, 24 F/A-18A Hornet, 10 A-6E Intruder, 10 S-3A/B Viking and 6 SH-3H Sea King; in support, 4 E-2C Hawkeye, 4 KA-6D tanker.
**Armament:** 3 BPDMS (Basic Point Defence Missile System) Mk 29 type, each with box of 8 NATO Sea Sparrow missiles; 3 20mm CIWS.

Above: Part of Carrier Task Force 77.7 in the South China Sea in January 1979; CG-16 Leahy, AFS-3 Niagara Falls and CV-64 Constellation. Distinctive shapes on the carrier's deck are 16 F-14A Tomcats with wings at max sweep.

Right: The main artwork depicts CV-64 Constellation as she was in the early 1980s. No two of the US Navy super-carriers look alike, and most can be distinguished visually at a distance. Note the four catapults, all aligned approximately fore and aft.

*Left: Since 1980 the CIWS (close-in weapon system) has been mass-produced and fitted to virtually every significant US Navy surface combatant. It comprises a self-contained radar-directed mount for an M61A1 aircraft-type six-barrel 20mm gun, firing at 3,000 rds/min, fed with high-density kinetic-energy penetrator ammunition to destroy aircraft or anti-ship missiles.*

*Right: An April 1983 picture of CV-66 America in the Indian Ocean, flying signal flags. On deck are Corsairs, Tomcats, Vikings, Intruders and Hawkeyes.*

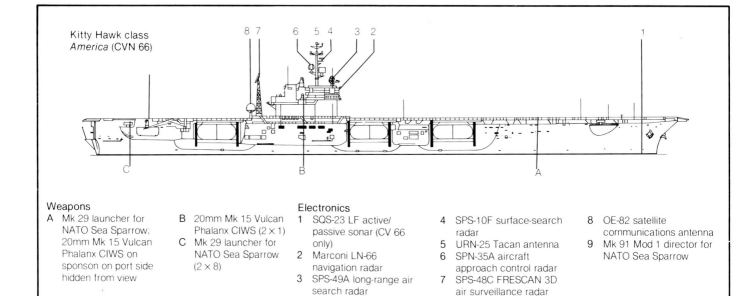

Kitty Hawk class
*America* (CVN 66)

**Weapons**

A  Mk 29 launcher for NATO Sea Sparrow; 20mm Mk 15 Vulcan Phalanx CIWS on sponson on port side hidden from view

B  20mm Mk 15 Vulcan Phalanx CIWS (2 × 1)

C  Mk 29 launcher for NATO Sea Sparrow (2 × 8)

**Electronics**

1  SQS-23 LF active/passive sonar (CV 66 only)
2  Marconi LN-66 navigation radar
3  SPS-49A long-range air search radar

4  SPS-10F surface-search radar
5  URN-25 Tacan antenna
6  SPN-35A aircraft approach control radar
7  SPS-48C FRESCAN 3D air surveillance radar

8  OE-82 satellite communications antenna
9  Mk 91 Mod 1 director for NATO Sea Sparrow

*Above: An ordnanceman of VA-97 pushes two Snakeyes across the deck of Constellation.*

*Left: A November 1977 picture of CV-63, the name ship of the class.*

*Right: An impressive aspect of the fourth ship of the class, CV-67 John F. Kennedy. She is slightly bigger than her sisters, and originally had different (Mk 25) missile launchers and fire control.*

The major visible differences are that the *John F Kennedy* has a canted stack — designed to keep the flight-deck clear of corrosive exhaust gases — and a flight deck of differently shaped forward end. The Terrier missile system, which consumed valuable space on the flight-deck and, in any case, duplicated similar area defence systems aboard the carrier escorts, was dropped in favour of the Mk 57 NATO Sea Sparrow missile System and has subsequently been deleted from the previous three ships.

These four ships are very powerful fighting units, second only to the US Navy's nuclear powered aircraft carriers in combat capability. However, all recent US Congresses have set their faces against anything but nuclear power for ships of this size, rejecting proposals for a CVV in 1979 and for a modified *John F Kennedy* in 1980, finally forcing the President to order a fourth Nimitz class CVN in the FY80 pro-

gramme. It would, therefore, seem that these four ships could be the last conventionally powered aircraft carriers to be built for the US Navy.

All four of these carriers are to be modernized under the US Navy's Service Life Extension programme (SLEP), *Kitty Hawk* was the first (July 21, 1987 to November 29, 1989) at a cost of $717 million, followed by *Constellation* (October 1989 to February 1992), *America* (April 1994 to August 1996) and finally *Kennedy* (July 1996 to November 1998). These 28-month refits will extend each ship's life by some 10-15 years. The work programme includes fitting new and more powerful catapults, updating the aircraft facilities, modernising all electronics and extensive refurbishment of the hull, propulsion systems and electrics. The *Kitty Hawk's* condition is so good that a less extensive and much cheaper SLEP than anticipated will be required.

# Midway

These ships were the last war-built US carriers. Three units were completed, but *Franklin D. Roosevelt* was stricken in 1977. As built, the Midway class had an axial flight deck with two centre-line lifts and a deck-edge lift amidships on the port side. The original design was quickly overtaken by developments in jet aircraft and the class underwent a major modernisation during the 1950s in which an 8-degree angled deck was constructed, the after lift moved to the deck edge position, C-11 catapults installed, and the armament reduced. *Coral Sea*, the last of the three to be modernised, incorporated a number of further modifications as a result of experience with her two sisters and with the Forrestal class. The port-side deck-edge lift was moved farther aft to clear the angled deck, and the forward centre-line lift replaced by a new deck-edge lift forward of the island. This conversion was particularly successful and *Coral Sea* remained largely unaltered throughout the 1960s and 1970s.

In 1966 *Midway* underwent a second major modernisation to enable her to operate the same aircraft as the more modern US carriers. The flight deck was completely rebuilt — its total area was increased by one third — and new lifts of greater capacity but similar in layout to those of *Coral Sea* installed. Two C-13 catapults were installed forward.

**Navy:** United States.
**Length:** 979ft (298.4m).
**Beam:** hull 121ft (36.9m).
**Draught:** 35.3ft (10.8m).
**Flight deck:** 945x238ft (288.72.5m); angled at 13°; 2 steam catapults.
**Displacement:** 51,000 tons standard; 62,200 full load.
**Propulsion:** 4 shafts; steam turbines, 212,000shp.
**Speed:** 33 knots (61km/h).
**Range:** 10,000nm (18,530km) at 20 knots.
**Crew:** 2,615 plus about 1,800 assigned to air wing.
**Air wing:** 24 F-14A/D Tomcat, 24 F/A-18A Hornet, 10 A-6E Intruder and 6 SH-3H Sea King; in support 4 E-2C Hawkeye, 4 KA-6D tanker.
**Armament:** 2 BPDMS (Basic Point Defence Missile Systems) Mk 25 launchers, each with box of Sea Sparrow missiles, plus 3 Mk 15 Phalanx 20mm CIWS.

BPDMS missile launchers replaced what remained of the original armament in 1979.

*Midway* was due to remain in service until 1988. *Coral Sea* had been reactivated to replace *Saratoga*, which was recently undergoing a Service Life Extension Program (SLEP), but she has subsequently become a training ship. Both ships are currently serving with the Pacific Fleet, and both operate as attack carriers, without fixed- or rotary-wing ASW aircraft.

*Right: Now serving as a training ship, CV-43 Coral Sea is seen here with F-4s, A-3s, A-7s and E-2s embarked.*

# Minas Gerais

Completed as the British light fleet carrier *Vengeance*, this vessel was purchased by Brazil in 1956 and refitted in Rotterdam. She emerged in 1960 with a flight deck angled at fully 8.5 degrees, a steam catapult, US radars and two new aircraft lifts. The catapult can launch aircraft weighing 30,000lb (13,640kg). In a refit 1976-81 a data link compatible with the data system of the large Niteroi-class ASW frigates was installed. Throughout her operational life *Minas Gerais* has served as an ASW carrier, with S-2 Tracker aircraft and helicopters: first the HSS-1 (SH-34) Seabat, then the larger SH-3 Sea King.

Throughout her active life with the Brazilian Navy this carrier has carried Pennant No A11, and has operated the Grumman Tracker ASW aircraft, initially in the S-2A form and more recently in the upgraded S-2E version. Brazil is one of the potential customers for Grumman's own scheme to update S-2s to Turbo Tracker standard with Garrett TPE331-1-AW turboprops.

**Navy:** Brazil.
**Length:** 695ft (211.8m).
**Beam:** hull 80ft (24.4m).
**Draught:** 24.5ft (7.5m).
**Flight deck:** 690x121ft (210.37m); angled at 8.5°; 1 steam catapult.
**Displacement:** 15,890 tons standard; 19,890 full load.
**Propulsion:** 2 shafts; steam turbines, 40,000shp.
**Speed:** 25.3 knots (46.9km/h).
**Range:** 12,000nm (22,240km) at 14 knots; 6,200 at 23 knots.
**Crew:** 1,005 plus 300 assigned to air group.
**Air group:** Maximum of 20, including 8 S-2E Tracker, 4 SH-3D Sea King, 2 Bell 206B and 2 UH-12 Esquilos (Ecureuils).
**Armament:** 2 quad 40mm AA guns and one twin 40mm AA.

Included in the modification package would be a totally new avionics and ASW sensor suite. Few changes would be needed in the ship, but it would enable the bunkers of 115-grade Avgas (petrol) to be eliminated, all aviation fuel then being standard Jet-A kerosene. The ship herself has long been in need of a major refit and upgrade, and should this be authorized it would probably be carried out at the Navyard, Rio de Janeiro.

*Right: Brazil's carrier, S-2s aboard, in 1972.*

# Moskva

Designated *protovolodchny kreyser* (anti-submarine cruiser) by the Soviet Navy, *Moskva* first appeared in 1967, followed by *Leningrad* in 1968, having been built in the Nosenko Yard in Nikolayev. The design of these two impressive-looking ships may have been influenced to a certain extent by the

helicopter cruisers built by the French and Italian navies during the early 1960s, such as the *Jeanne d'Arc* and *Vittorio Veneto,* but the Soviet ships are much larger and able to operate an air group of up to 18 aircraft. They also helped to serve notice on the West that the Soviet Navy was starting to move into the ship-borne aviation business in a big way.

There is no doubt that the principal mission for which these two ships were designed was to hunt and destroy US Navy Polaris SSBNs in the eastern Mediterranean. However, they have played a major role introducing large-scale air operations to the Soviet Navy and in training ships' officers, crew and aviators in the techniques of operating large numbers of aircraft from shipborne platforms. They have thus served as stepping-stones to the *Kiev,* and ultimately to the Kremlin class aircraft carriers.

The air group comprises 15-18 Ka-25 Hormones housed in a spacious hangar beneath the half-length flight deck. This is served by two aircraft lifts, which are somewhat narrow and limit operational deployments to Hormones. This was demonstrated clearly when *Leningrad* deployed to the Suez Canal area in the summer of 1974 with Mi-8s Hips: these

**Navy:** Soviet Union.
**Length:** 624.8ft (190.5m).
**Beam:** (waterline) 85.3ft (26m).
**Draught:** 24.9ft (7.6m).
**Flight deck:** 295.3x115ft (90x35m) axial no catapult.
**Displacement:** 14,500 tons standard; 18,000 full load.
**Propulsion:** 2 shafts; steam turbines, 100,000shp.
**Speed:** Over 30 knots (55.6km/h).
**Range:** not accurately known, but over 10,000nm (18,530km).
**Crew:** 770 plus 70 assigned to air group.
**Air group:** Up to 18 helicopters, now of Kamov Ka-27 "Helix" type, in different versions.
**Armament:** 4 57mm dual-purpose guns, 2 twin SA-N-3 (SAM) missile installations, 2 12-tube MBU-2500A ASW rocket launchers, 10 21in (533mm) torpedo tubes.

*Below: Moskva in the Med in 1970, when her pennant number was 841 (these numbers are frequently changed by the Soviets).*

Below: Moskva class ASW cruisers carry an air wing of 16 Kamov Ka-25 Hormone-As (shown here) and two Hormone-Bs. The ASW version, Hormone-A, is fitted with a chin radome, dipping sonar and sonobuoys and carries depth charges or torpedoes. Hormone-B has a video data link system for over-the-horizon targeting.

Below: SA-N-3 Goblet missiles and twin-arm launcher. This missile has a range of 32,800 yards (30,000m) and an interception altitude of 300ft (91m) to 80,000ft (24,400m). Missile control is by the Headlight director. These are huge installations, superimposed at the front of the superstructure, one for each launcher.

Above: Soviet aircraft designers receive credit and publicity for the work, but their naval designer compatriots are anonymous men who recieve no publicity. Yet they must be remarkable people, as many of their ship designs are so daring and full of original ideas. An early example of their skills is the Moskva class air-capable ASW cruiser, which combines a large, uncluttered flight deck aft with a heavy and effective armament forward and a varied and apparently comprehensive sensor fit.

were too large for the lifts and could not be struck down into the hangar.

The primary ASW weapons system of the Moskvas is the Ka-25 helicopter, which is normally of the Hormone-A ASW type, although some of the -B version are also carried. Unlike Western aircraft carriers at the time they were designed, the forward part of these Soviet ships is occupied by a comprehensive weapons outfit of ASW and air defence systems. There is a twin SUW-N-1 anti-submarine missile launcher on the forecastle, and two RBU-6000 rocket launchers in the bow. There is also an SA-N-3 area air defence system, and two twin 57mm dual-purpose gun-mountings seem to have been fitted almost as an afterthought.

ASW sensors include a hull-mounted LF sonar and a stern-mounted VDS. As built, the two ships had torpedo tubes mounted in line with the bridge and just above the water-line. These have since been removed, almost certainly because they must have been inoperable in any sort of seaway. The tall, pyramid-shaped superstructure includes the bridge, funnel and numerous radio, radar and ESM antennas.

*Moskva* was used in 1973 for the carrier trials of the Yak-38 Forger. No operational deployment has ever taken place with this V/STOL aircraft, possibly because of the limitations imposed by the lifts.

The two units of the class built, *Moskva* and *Leningrad*, have served the Soviet Navy well. However, Soviet interest in medium-sized air-capable ships seems to have waned in favour of the much larger ships of the Kiev-class.

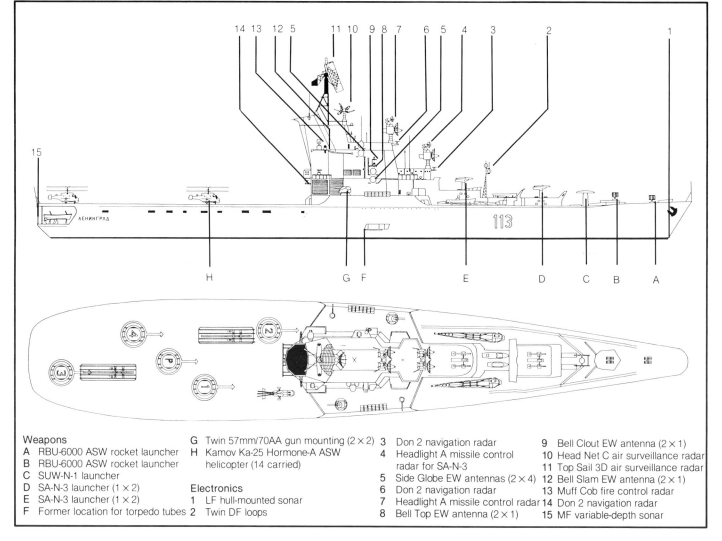

Weapons
A  RBU-6000 ASW rocket launcher
B  RBU-6000 ASW rocket launcher
C  SUW-N-1 launcher
D  SA-N-3 launcher (1 × 2)
E  SA-N-3 launcher (1 × 2)
F  Former location for torpedo tubes

G  Twin 57mm/70AA gun mounting (2 × 2)
H  Kamov Ka-25 Hormone-A ASW helicopter (14 carried)

Electronics
1  LF hull-mounted sonar
2  Twin DF loops

3  Don 2 navigation radar
4  Headlight A missile control radar for SA-N-3
5  Side Globe EW antennas (2 × 4)
6  Don 2 navigation radar
7  Headlight A missile control radar
8  Bell Top EW antenna (2 × 1)

9  Bell Clout EW antenna (2 × 1)
10  Head Net C air surveillance radar
11  Top Sail 3D air surveillance radar
12  Bell Slam EW antenna (2 × 1)
13  Muff Cob fire control radar
14  Don 2 navigation radar
15  MF variable-depth sonar

*Right: Moskva has herself recently used pennant numbers 841, 847, 854 (as here) and 857. It is unusual for these ships to make such dense smoke, though they do have oil-fired water-tube boilers. Even Soviet gas-turbine driven warships often make quite a lot of smoke.*

*Below: Over 150 men, most stripped to the waist, were marching round Moskva's flight deck when a Royal Navy helicopter took this picture in September 1979. In the background is a "Kara" cruiser.*

# Nimitz

The Nimitz class aircraft carriers are the mightiest and most powerful warships in history. Each ship normally carries some 90 aircraft whose capabilities range from nuclear strike, through interception and ground-attack to close-in anti-submarine protection — a more powerful and better balanced tactical air force than many national air forces. Each carrier is manned by a crew of 3,300 with an air wing of a further 3,000. And their nuclear reactors have cores which enable them to operate for thirteen years at a stretch, equivalent to steaming up to one million miles.

Such extraordinary statistics will only be challenged when the Soviet Navy's nuclear-powered supercarriers enter service in the 1990s, and it is, in fact, the perceived threat from the Nimitz class that has caused such massive development in the Soviet Navy over the past 15 years.

The original nuclear-powered carrier, USS *Enterprise* (CVN 65), commissioned in 1961, was built in the remarkably short time of 45 months and was so successful that, when the time came to plan a replacement for the Midway class, nuclear power was the preferred means of propulsion. The advances that had been made meant that the eight A2W reactors used in *Enterprise* (each producing 35,000shp) could be replaced by just two A4W reactors, each producing approximately 130,000shp. In addition, the uranium cores need to be replaced much less frequently than those originally used in *Enterprise*.

This reduction in the number of reactors also permitted major improvements in the internal arrangements below hangar deck level. In *Enterprise* the entire centre section of the ship is occupied by machinery rooms, with the aviation

**Navy:** United States.
**Length:** 1,092ft (332.8m).
**Beam:** 134ft (40.8m).
**Draught:** 37ft (11.3m).
**Flight deck:** 1,092x252ft (332.8x76.8m), increasing by 5ft (1.5m) on 3rd ship, *Theodore Roosevelt*, 4 catapults.
**Displacement:** 81,600 tons standard; 91,487 full load.
**Propulsion:** 4 shafts; steam turbines nuclear boiler heat, 280,000shp.
**Speed:** Over 30 knots (55.5km/h).
**Crew:** 3,300 ship, plus 3,000 air wing.
**Launched:** 1972.
**Commissioned:** 1975.
**Air wing:** 24 F-14A Tomcat; 24 A-7E Corsair, 10 A-6E Intruder plus 4 KA-6D; 4 E-2C Hawkeye; 4EA-6B Prowler; 10 S-3A Viking; plus 6 SH-3H Sea King helicopters.
**Armament:** 3 Mk 25 Basic Point Defence Missile System (BPDMS) launchers with Sea Sparrow missiles; being replaced by Mk29 launcher for NATO Sea Sparrow; plus 3 Phalanx CIWS guns.

*Right: When the Sparrow AAM was hastily adopted as a naval SAM it was fitted in its existing (1963) AIM-7E form into a modified ASROC (anti-submarine rocket) eight-cell launcher, which became the BPMDS Mk 25 launch system aboard many ships including the carriers Forrestal, Saratoga, Independence, Midway, Coral Sea, JFK, Enterprise and Nimitz. From 1974 Mk 25 was replaced by the lightweight Mk 29 launcher matched to the RIM-7H and RIM-7M Sparrows with folding wings and fins as part of the NATO Sea Sparrow system. Today all CVs/CVNs have the Mk 29.*

*Right: Both Nimitz, seen here, and the second ship of the class, Dwight D. Eisenhower, were ordered as CVANs (attack carriers), but in the summer of 1975, soon after Nimitz commissioned, they were redesignated as CVNs. This involved adding a control centre and other facilities for anti-submarine aircraft (S-3A/S-3B and S-3H). These were provided from the start in the remaining ships, CVN-70 Carl Vinson, CVN-71 Theodore Roosevelt, CVN-72 Abraham Lincoln and CVN-73 George Washington.*

*Left: The main drawing depicts the third ship of the class, CVN-70 Carl Vinson. In the foreground can be seen the projecting sponson carrying the Mk 29 NATO Sea Sparrow launcher and Phalanx CIWS. The very first Sea Sparrow (Mk 25) launcher was installed on Forrestal in this location, but most subsequent carriers had only two launchers, both at the stern (at first America and Constellation had no Sea Sparrow, but two twin launchers for the bigger Terrier).*

fuel compartments and the missile magazines pushed out towards the end of the ship, but in *Nimitz* the propulsion machinery is divided into two separate units with the magazines between and forward of them. The improved layout has resulted in an increase of 20 per cent in aviation fuel capacity and a similar increase in the volume available for munitions and stores. The flight-deck layout for the Nimitz class is almost identical to that of the *John F Kennedy* (CV 67) of the Kitty Hawk class.

The provision of defensive weapons and sensors on the first two — *Nimitz* (CVN 68) and *Eisenhower* (CVN 69) — was initially on a par with that on the *John F Kennedy* (CV 67), although the third ship, *Carl Vinson* (CVN 70), has NATO Sea Sparrow and Phalanx in place of the BPDMS launchers on earlier ships, which have been similarly fitted during refits. This parallels the increase in defensive armament taking place on the carriers of other navies. *Vinson* is also fitted with an ASW control centre and specialized maintenance facilities for the S-3 Viking; these have also been installed in *Nimitz* and *Eisenhower* in the course of refits.

*Right: The third ship of the class, Vinson, at sea. In many respects she was the first definitive member of the family, fully equipped from the drawing board for all kinds of oceanic air warfare including ASW.*

*Below: Looking down on the JFK, CV-67. Though a member of an earlier class (63 Kitty Hawk, 64 Constellation, 66 America and this ship) CV-67 is generally very similar to the Nimitz family, differing mainly in being slightly smaller and using oil fuel. She has three Mk 29 launchers.*

*Below right: This outline diagram shows main features of the class including the four elevators (three on the starboard side), three Mk 29 launchers, four catapults and principal electronic antennas.*

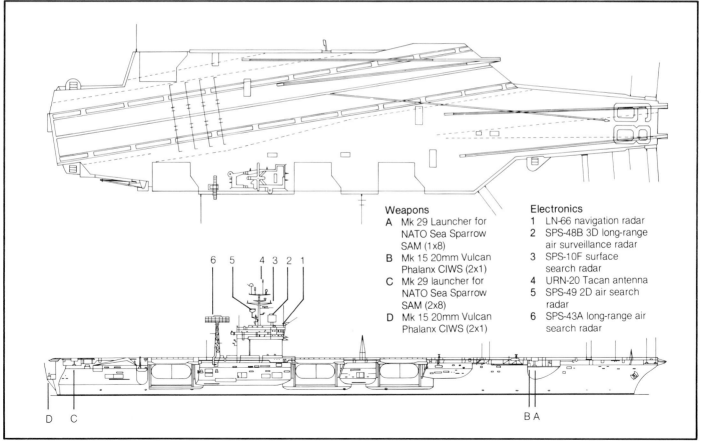

**Weapons**

A  Mk 29 Launcher for
   NATO Sea Sparrow
   SAM (1x8)
B  Mk 15 20mm Vulcan
   Phalanx CIWS (2x1)
C  Mk 29 launcher for
   NATO Sea Sparrow
   SAM (2x8)
D  Mk 15 20mm Vulcan
   Phalanx CIWS (2x1)

**Electronics**

1  LN-66 navigation radar
2  SPS-48B 3D long-range
   air surveillance radar
3  SPS-10F surface
   search radar
4  URN-20 Tacan antenna
5  SPS-49 2D air search
   radar
6  SPS-43A long-range air
   search radar

Delays in construction caused by shipyard problems resulted in rocketing costs and in the late 1970s the Carter Administration attempted unsuccessfully to block authorization funds for the construction of a fourth carrier in favour of a smaller (50,000 ton), conventionally-powered design, known as the CVV. However, the CVV was never popular with the US Navy, and the Reagan Administration has now committed itself to the continuation of the CVN programme.

Current deployment has *Nimitz* and *Eisenhower* in the Atlantic and *Vinson* in the Pacific, but when the *Roosevelt* was commissioned late in 1986 she joined the Atlantic Fleet, releasing *Nimitz* for a move to the Pacific Fleet, balancing the CVN force.

The two carriers of this class under construction — *Abraham Lincoln* (CVN 72) and *George Washington* (CVN 73) — are scheduled to be commissioned in late 1990 and 1991 respectively, and when the last is commissioned the USS *Coral Sea* (CV 43), a Midway class carrier commissioned in 1947, will be retired from the front-line force to become a training carrier.

*Above: An F-14 Tomcat has just been launched from Vinson, and a pair of A-7Es await their turn. At that time the only Tomcat was the F-14A, which needs full afterburner for take off. Today the much superior F-14A Plus and F-14D have F110 engines so powerful that aircraft can be launched in dry thrust. Today the A-7E is being replaced by the F/A-18A and C, and in the 1990s the long-lived A-6E Intruder is expected to be replaced by the A-12A Advanced Tactical Aircraft.*

*Left: Inside the Air Traffic Control Centre of CVN-69 Dwight D. Eisenhower. This great ship has always served with the Atlantic Fleet, chiefly with the Sixth Fleet in the Mediterranean. In this busy theatre she has often been the centre of much activity, notably off Libya and the Lebanon. As this book went to press everyone was wondering how such sophisticated ships could (the US Navy states) mistake an Iran Air Airbus for a hostile attacking fighter.*

*Right: Bow-on view of the "Ike" (popular name for the great soldier Eisenhower and the ship named after him). Incidentally, no other US Navy ship has been named for an officer in the US Army.*

# Principe de Asturias

This ship, striking because of its prominent ski-jump, was based on the US Navy's SCS (Sea Control Ship), which was planned in 1960-73. Planned as a neat, modern multirole vessel, with advanced electronics and a range of weapons for many duties, the SCS was finally abandoned by the US Navy, but not by Spain. The latter purchased the rights to the design, and with the assistance of New York design firm Gibbs and Cox, and of Dixencast, they built the "PA-11" themselves at the Bazán yard at El Ferrol from 1980. It had been planned to commission the ship in 1984, but though she was launched in May 1982 her fitting out took a long time. In the end she began sea trials in November 1987 (it was proudly proclaimed this was "40 days ahead of schedule").

An austere ship, intended chiefly for ASW and air-superiority operations in low-threat areas, she has a single COGAG (combined gas turbine and gas turbine) propulsion system, with two LM2500 sets putting the power into a single screw. The after two-thirds of the ship comprises a single full-width hangar, and it is claimed that 37 aircraft could be embarked if necessary. A more likely mix is 6/8 EAV-8B Harrier IIs, 6/8 SH-3Ds and up to 8 LAMPS III or Vertrep helicopters.

The first three of 12 EAV-8Bs flew non-stop from St Louis to Rota in October 1987, and all had been delivered by spring 1988. By this time the ship's sea trials had been completed, and her SPS-55 surface radar was functioning.

Commissioned in May 1988, the new STOVL-carrier will become the nucleus of a fully operational battle group by late 1989, including four newly built *Santa Maria* (FFG-7 type) escorting frigates. The EAV-8Bs are based closely on the US Marine Corps Harrier IIs, and the LAMPS III S-70Bs are based on the SH-60Bs of the US Navy.

**Navy:** Spain.
**Length:** 643ft (196m).
**Beam:** 80ft (24.4m).
**Draught:** 30ft (9.1m).
**Flight deck:** 574x105ft (175x32m); 12° ski-jump; no catapults.
**Displacement:** 16,200 tons full load.
**Propulsion:** 2 gas turbines, 1 shaft; 46,000hp.
**Speed:** 26 knots (48km/h).
**Crew:** 774 ship, plus air group.
**Launched:** 1982.
**Commissioned:** 1988.
**Air group:** Accommodation for: 6 to 8 EAV-8B (Harrier IIs); 6 to 8 Sea King or S-70B helicopters; 8 AB 212 helicopters; maximum 20 aircraft.
**Armament:** Published so far: 4 12-barrel Meroka 20mm rapid-fire (CIWS) gun mounts; plus ECM chaff launchers. (Aircraft planned can of course carry wide range of air-to-air and ASW weapons).

*Below: In sharpest contrast to the aircraft carriers serving with most of the world's minor navies, this vessel is new from the keel up, and carefully designed to meet the requirements of today. Her design is basically American, as is her equipment which includes General Electric propulsion gas turbines and a digital command and control system. Her range is estimated at 6,500nm (12,050km) at 20 knots, which is appreciably more than that of the other vessels making up the planned combat group. Armament details had not been published in summer 1988.*

*Above right: The clean and shapely lines of the new carrier are seen in this picture taken shortly after the launch at El Ferrol. Bazán has built 1,000 warships since 1730.*

*Right: The Spanish Navy's adoption of the SCS (Sea Control Ship) concept shows great imagination, particularly as this represents an economical alternative to the conventional carrier. This medium-sized aircraft carrier with full-length flight-deck, but operating STOVL aircraft, offers the most realistic way of taking air power to sea in an era of rapidly escalating costs. The port side elevation drawing of Príncipe de Asturias clearly shows the prominent 12° ski-jump on the bows, while the plan view drawing, showing the 574 x 105ft (175 x 32m) full-length flight-deck, gives a clear idea of the austere lines of the vessel.*

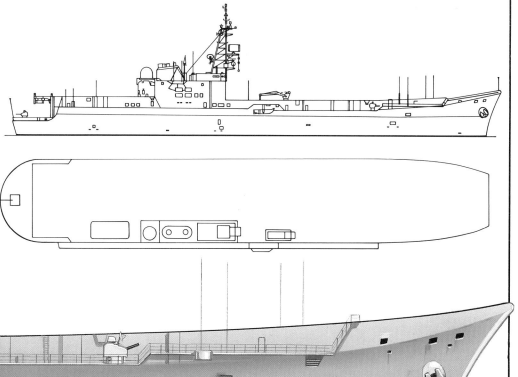

# Vikrant

Laid down as the British light fleet carrier *Hercules,* this vessel was incomplete when purchased by India in 1957. An angled deck was fitted, together with a steam catapult and mirror landing sight, before *Vikrant* was finally handed over in 1961. She was partially air-conditioned and, as insulation for the tropical climate in which she would operate, the ship's sides were sprayed with asbestos cement. The hangar, which is centrally located with the two aircraft lifts at either end, is 445ft long and 52ft wide (135.6m x 15.8m).

From her completion *Vikrant* has served as an attack carrier, operating Sea Hawk jet fighter-bombers and a handful of Alizé turbo-prop ASW aircraft. In 1979 she was taken in hand for a major modernisation which included the replacement of boilers and engines and the installation of new sensors and a combat information centre. She de-commissioned again in mid-1983 when a "ski jump" was constructed for the Sea Harrier aircraft ordered as replacements for the Sea Hawk.

Altogether, 24 Sea Harriers were ordered, but the last eight will equip INS *Viraat,* ex-*Hermes.* After reconstruction *Vikrant* is scheduled to remain in service for a further ten years, although the *Alizés* may not last that long.

Above: One of the first batch of six BAe Sea Harrier FRS.51s being demonstrated at Farnborough prior to delivery. India is the only export customer for the battle-proven "FRS".

Right: Even before delivery the Indian Sea Harriers carried the tail badge of No 300 (White Tiger) Squadron. The Sea Harrier is described in the aircraft section of this book.

Navy: India.
Length: 700ft (213.4m).
Beam: hull 80ft (24.4m).
Draught: 24ft (7.3m).
Flight deck: 700x128ft (213.4x39m); angled at 6°; 1 steam catapult.
Displacement: 16,000 tons standard; 19,500 full load.
Propulsion: 2 shafts; steam turbines, 40,000shp.
Speed: 24.5 knots (45.4km/h).
Range: 12,000nm (22,240km) at 14 knots.
Crew: (war complement) 1,345 including air group personnel.
Air group: Typically 8 Sea Harrier FRS.51 and 6 Alizé ASW aircraft, sometimes accompanied by Chetak (Alouette III) helicopters.
Armament: 4 twin and 7 single 40mm AA.

Below: Side elevation of INS Vikrant, showing the ski-jump in the bows which was added in a refit in 1983-84. She is a considerably smaller ship than INS Viraat (formerly HMS Hermes), but she is a close relative of Argentina's 25 de Mayo.

Inset right: Plan view of Vikrant showing her traditional layout, with centreline elevators (aircraft lifts) and no major overhang for the angled deck, which in consequence is restricted to 6° Black dots denote four of the single 40mm guns.

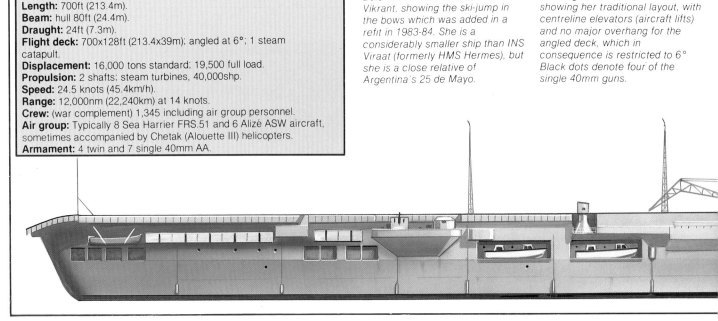

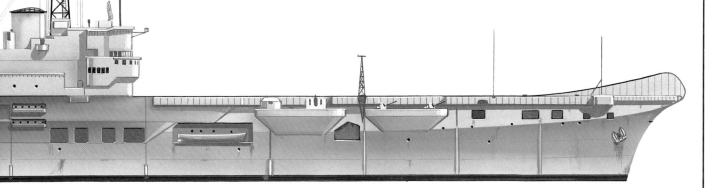

SEA-BASED air power has five primary roles: anti-submarine warfare (ASW), strike/attack, air defence (AD), electronic warfare (EW) and airborne early warning (AEW). Airframes divide into three obvious categories: conventional take-off and landing (CTOL), fixed-wing vertical/short take off and landing (V/STOL) and helicopters.

ASW tasks are performed by CTO aircraft ranging from the four-place Lockheed S-3 Viking operating with the US Navy to the many types of helicopter such as the Soviet Kamov Ka-27 Helix and the US Sikorsky SH-60B Seahawk. The principal requirements of a CTOL ASW aircraft are to be able to transit economically and then spend as much time as possible on patrol, during which it must be able to detect, locate, identify and finally destroy submarine targets. This necessitates a variety of on-board sensors including radar (for detection and classification of surface targets), forward-looking infra-red (FLIR), magnetic anomaly detectors (MAD), sonobuoys and electronic countermeasures (ECM) equipment. All these sensors, plus inputs from the parent carrier, and from other ships and aircraft, produce so much information that considerable on-board processing power is necessary.

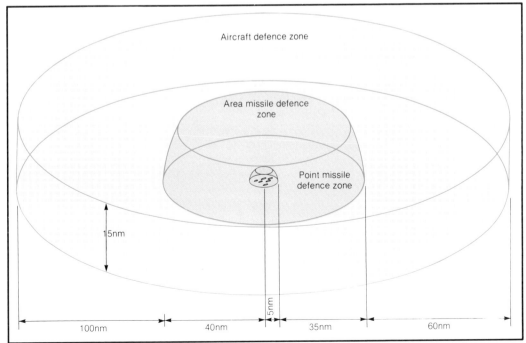

Above: The latest and by far the most costly shipboard helicopter to enter service in the West is the Sikorsky SH-60B Seahawk, seen here landing aboard the frigate USS Crommelin in 1983.

Far left: Newest and most versatile CTOL fixed- airpower at sea is the McDonnell F/A-18A Hornet, seen here with US Marine squadron VMFA-514. Such airpower demands steam catapults and arrester gear.

Left: A theoretical representation of the air defence zones around a modern US Navy Carrier Battle Group. The ships are at the centre. Point Missiles (Sea Sparrow) give last-ditch protection to about 3nm, as does the Phalanx ''Gatling gun''. Area Missiles (Standard) protect to a radius of 35nm, while aircraft (F-14s) defend within a radius of 100nm (115 miles, 185km). ASW and attack aircraft would be effective out to much greater distances.

To attack its targets the aircraft also obviously needs a weapon load which ideally would include missiles for use against surface targets (Exocet, Harpoon, for example), as well as homing torpedoes, rockets and conventional/nuclear depth bombs. The only CTOL aircraft currently capable of performing the complete ASW task is the S-3 Viking. The Soviet Navy will probably produce a similar type of ASW aircraft when its new 75,000 ton carrier enters service.

An alternative to the CTOL ASW aircraft, albeit with less range/endurance, is the helicopter. This has been developed from a simple extension of the parent ship's sensors (with a real-time down-link) to a fully autonomous weapon system in its own right. Further, it has had the exceptional advantage of bringing an air capability to ships down to frigate size. The most advanced design in this category is the EHI EH-101, a British/Italian Sea King replacement. Not yet in service, this aircraft will be equipped with Ferranti Blue Kestrel search radar, Marconi sonar systems, Decca ESM (electronic sup-

port measures) and AN/AQS-81 MAD, all brought together by a Ferranti data-handling system.

Strike/attack roles are performed primarily by fixed-wing aircraft, using missiles, bombs or rockets. As so dramatically demonstrated in the South Atlantic War, a fast jet aircraft such as the French-built Super Etendard armed with Exocet sea-skimming missiles is a potentially lethal combination. Such an attack is feasible also by US aircraft armed with Harpoon missiles (Grumman A-6 Intruder, S-3 Viking), and the British Sea Harrier with Harpoon or Sea Eagle. The Soviet Navy currently has no capability in this area (from sea-based aircraft), but it must be presumed that they are developing a suitable aircraft/missile combination for service on the new carriers. Helicopters can also carry ASMs, and the French Super Frelon carrying AM.39 Exocets has been used by Iraq in the Gulf War with some success, while the British Lynx used Sea Skuas against (surfaced) submarines and surface ships in the South Atlantic War.

*Left: Apart from the dual-role F/A-18 the only attack aircraft in service with US Navy carrier air wings is the Grumman A-6E Intruder, seen here with TRAM (target recognition attack multisensor) turret under the nose for night attacks.*

*Right: Most efficient of the shipboard anti-ship helicopters, the Westland Lynx is seen here armed with four Sea Skua missiles, which home on signals reflected from the target illuminated by the helicopter's Seaspray radar.*

*Below: Arrival of the Lockheed S-3A Viking aboard US Navy carriers (seen here, final trials aboard USS Enterprise in 1974) gave carriers a total ASW capability using their own aircraft. Today this capability is to be upgraded with the SH-60F.*

## Airborne air defence

Air defence by aircraft is a role confined to fixed-wing types, of which the technically most advanced is the Grumman F-14 Tomcat. Operating from the US larger CVNs, the F-14 also performs the reconnaissance role. The Sea Harrier demonstrated its air defence capabilities in the South Atlantic where it was responsible for shooting down in air-to-air combat eleven Mirages, eight A-4 Skyhawks, one Canberra, one Pucara and one C-131 Hercules. The only Soviet air defence aircraft is the Yak-36 "Forger", a fixed-wing VTOL machine which has limited capabilities.

In the area of specialised EW aircraft the only machine currently in service is the US Navy's Grumman EA-6 Prowler, a remarkable design with a comprehensive ECM/ESM capability. No other naval air arm has attempted to produce such a sophisticated (and extremely expensive) aircraft type.

In the South Atlantic War it was demonstrated that radar picket ships are an inadequate substitute for an airborne

early-warning system. The only effective type currently in service is the Grumman E-2C Hawkeye, a twin-turboprop aircraft, which establishes a patrol some 200nm (370km) from its parent carrier, where its powerful APS-125 radar has considerable range. The British have produced an AEW version of the ubiquitous Westland Sea King helicopter, equipped with a Searchwater radar (as used on the Nimrod), mounted in an inflatable radome on the starboard side of the aircraft. Conceived in haste, this has proved an effective solution to the problem, although less economical than a fixed-wing CTOL aircraft.

The current Soviet practice of long-range land-based AEW for its naval task groups will doubtless prove vulnerable and inadequate in war and they will almost certainly have to develop a carrier-borne AEW aircraft to make their new task groups fully effective. The same also applies to the French Navy, whose new CVNs would inevitably be high-value targets in any naval conflict, and highly vulnerable without an AEW aircraft.

*Left: As a carrier battle group (task force) can move 500 miles (800km) a day it is difficult to attack using long-range missiles, unless these have some homing capability. It follows that carrier-based fighters play a crucial role, and from 1972 until after 2000 the chief US Navy fighter is the Grumman F-14 Tomcat. Hardly ever changed except to update the avionics, the biggest improvement (in the F-14A Plus and F-14D) is the new GE F110 engine. This gives much better reliability and so much extra power that launches can be made without afterburner.*

*Right: For political reasons which Britain did away with conventional carriers (the last was paid off in 1978) and instead built three small and simple ships called "through-deck cruisers". Eventually these were permitted to carry Sea Harriers, but the original purpose of these ships was to carry ASW helicopters of which the latest (until the EH101 becomes available) are these Westland Sea King HAS.5s. Each has totally autonomous ASW capability, with self-contained navaids, ASW sensors and processors, torpedoes and electronic support measures. Here a crew of four goes aboard.*

# BAe Sea Harrier

With the phasing out of large-deck carriers during the 1970s, the Through-Deck Cruiser (TDC) would be the only air-capable ship on the drawing board, and she was designed to operate only ASW helicopters from a flight deck of modest dimensions, without catapults or arrester wires. The only possibility of ensuring a continuation of fixed-wing operations in the Royal Navy therefore lay in V/STOL aircraft. Even so, the decision to order the Sea Harrier was taken only in 1975, when *Invincible* had already been under construction for three years.

The Sea Harrier is basically an RAF GR.3 with a marinised Pegasus Mk 103 engine (designated Mk 104) and a completely redesigned forward fuselage. The cockpit was raised 11in (280mm) to provide increased space for mission avionics, and a fuller canopy was adopted to improve rearward visibility. The nose was enlarged to accommodate a Ferranti Blue Fox multi-mode radar which can operate in the airborne search and intercept, and the air-to-surface search and strike modes. The changes from the basic Harrier design reflect in part the need for the Sea Harrier to operate in a maritime environment, but also a change of role from close support to fleet air defence and maritime strike (hence the FRS — Fighter Reconnaissance Strike — designation). Aluminium alloys were substituted for magnesium components in order to combat salt corrosion, an emergency braking system installed, and tie-down lugs provided on the undercarriage. The weapon hardpoints were strengthened with new ejection release units, and a missile control panel was installed in the cockpit for handling AIM-9 Sidewinder AAMs (outer wing pylons) and Harpoon/Sea Eagle ASMs (inner pylons). The development of the 'ski jump' ramp has provided considerable payload benefits when a short rolling take-off is employed.

Initial Royal Navy orders were for 34 aircraft, and no less than 28 of these saw service in the South Atlantic during the Falklands conflict. The Sea Harrier was used extensively in the fleet air defence role, armed with Sidewinder AAMs on the outer pylons and with drop tanks on the inner

pylons to improve combat radius, and was also employed in the land attack role. Six aircraft were lost (two to ground fire and the others in flying accidents), and these have been replaced by new construction, an additional seven aircraft being ordered at the same time to make up the third carrier air squadron. The only other nation so far to purchase the Sea Harrier is India, which has ordered 16 FRS.51s plus three T.60 trainers to replace Sea Hawks on the carrier *Vikrant* and eight FRS. 51s for the *Viraat* (ex-HMS *Hermes*).

*Right: Sea Harriers need no catapult. Here an FRS.1 launches from an Invincible class ship.*

*Below: Sea Harriers make VLs (vertical landings) during the Falklands war. They were fitted with 190gal drop tanks and twin AIM-9L launchers.*

# Breguet Alizé

In 1948 initial design work began in France on a home-grown carrier-based strike aircraft, which became the Vultur (Br. 960). An unusual configuration was adopted, with a Rolls-Royce Nene jet at the back and a turboprop in the nose — an arrangement designed to provide a good combat radius (using only the turboprop) combined with high performance in the strike area. The Vultur was not proceeded with, and in 1954 it was decided to convert it into an anti-submarine aircraft. The turbojet was replaced by a retractable radome, and sonobuoys were located in two wing nacelles. An internal weapons bay can accommodate a homing torpedo or depth bombs, and there are also eight underwing pylons for additional ordnance. The pilot and a radar operator sit side by side beneath a broad cockpit canopy, and there is a second systems operator in a side-facing seat behind them.

Seventy-five Alizés were built for the carriers *Clemenceau* and *Foch*, and 20 of these remain in service with 4F and 6F. Twelve Alizés were also delivered to India for service aboard the carrier *Vikrant*. The Alizé has proved successful and reliable in service, but no replacement is envisaged by the French. Twenty-eight aircraft have now been modernised to keep them in service until the end of the decade. An Iguane sea radar and a new acoustics processor have been fitted. The Alizés in service with the Indian Navy are also to be updated while the carrier *Vikrant* undergoes modernisation.

*Right: A fine view of an Alizé of France's Aéronavale coming in over the stern of a carrier. The engine is a 1,975hp RR Dart 21.*

*Below: Another French Alizé about to pick up a wire. France is building new carriers and will probably buy an Alizé successor.*

## Dassault-Breguet Rafale M

In 1983 Dassault-Breguet decided to build the prototype of a completely new multi-role fighter known as the Rafale (Squall). This aircraft first flew on 4 July 1986. Like other new fighters it has a large delta (triangular) wing, with squared-off tips for missile rails, a forward canard foreplane and twin engines fed from inlets under the fuselage. In the absence of any other engines the prototype is powered by General Electric F404 augmented turbofans of about 16,000lb (7258kg) thrust each. The prototype soon achieved a Mach number of 2, and in April 1987 it carried out a series of approaches to a French carrier, but without landing.

In 1988 the company received the go-ahead for the proposed production versions, the Rafale D for the Armée de l'Air, and the Rafale M for the

Aéronavale for operation from the two nuclear-powered carriers planned to commission by the end of the century. Compared with the prototype the production aircraft will be slightly smaller, and it is hoped to be lighter with an empty weight of only 18,960lb (8,600kg). The engines will be two SNECMA M88 turbofans of 16,860lb (7650kg) thrust each. The M version will be equipped for nose-tow catapult launch and arrested landing, and a 'mini ski-jump' has also been suggested (presumably in connection with free takeoffs). It will have an RDX radar and comprehensive other avionics for air combat, surface attack and other missions. Weapons will include a 30mm gun and six or eight missiles including MICA short-range and AMRAAM medium-range "fire and forget" weapons.

Above: The Rafale prototype is seen here carrying Magic II AAMs on the wingtips and four dummy MICA missiles on fuselage. Rafale is in direct competition with Eurofighter EFA.

## Dassault-Breguet Super Etendard

The original Etendard IV was developed as a light 'strike fighter' to operate from the carriers *Foch* and *Clemenceau*. Sixty-nine of the IVM attack version and 21 of the IVP photo-reconnaissance variant were built, and two mixed squadrons of Etendard aircraft, each comprising eight IVM plus two IVP, served on both French carriers until the late 1970s. It was first envisaged that the Etendard would be replaced by a navalised Jaguar, but following the cancellation of this project on political and cost grounds it was decided to opt for an improved Etendard, which became the Super Etendard. Flight development using three converted Etendard IVs took place 1974-77, and the Super Etendard began replacing the IVM (but not the IVP, which remains in service) in first-line squadrons in 1979. The airframe of the Super Etendard has been substantially redesigned for higher airspeeds and weights, and a new, more efficient engine and inertial navigation system were produced in France with US help. The Agarve multi-mode radar was developed for the low-level surface attack role, for which the Super Etendard is fitted with the AM.39 Exocet missile. The aircraft also has a nuclear strike capability.

Initially 100 aircraft were to have been purchased for the Aéronavale, but the order was subsequently cut to 71, 36 of which now serve in three *flotilles* — 11F, 14F, and 17F. In 1979 Argentina ordered 14 Super Etendards to replace the A-4Q Skyhawks aboard its carrier *25 de Mayo* and although only five had been delivered by April 1982 these quickly made their mark on the Falklands conflict, sinking both the destroyer *Sheffield* and the container ship *Atlantic Conveyor* with Exocet missiles. From 1991 the Aéronavale force will be upgraded with Anemone radar, a new inertial platform and computer, new HUD and modernised cockpit.

*Right: ASMP has now been integrated with the French Aéronavale Super Etendards, but for some time the chief stand-off weapon will remain the AM39 Exocet, as used by Argentine Super Etendards in 1982.*

*Above right: The newest weapon carried by French Super Etendards is ASMP nuclear cruise missile which can fly to a target at a range of up to 155 miles, (250km).*

# Grumman A-6 Intruder

The A-6 Intruder was designed from the outset as an all-weather medium attack aircraft. It is fitted with the DIANE (Digital Integrated Attack Navigation Equipment) system, which enables the entire flight mission to be flown without visual reference.

The model in current service with the US Navy and the Marine Corps is the A-6E which introduced a new multi-mode radar and a new computer. A total of 159 new-built A-6Es were purchased, and a further 240 A-6As were modfied to the same standard. The A-6E has been constantly updated, the latest addition being TRAM (Target Recognition Attack Multisensor), a turreted electro-optical system designed for use in blind precision attack, if necessary with laser-guided weapons. Intruders are currently being modified to fire the Harpoon

anti-ship missile, the first Harpoon-capable aircraft being deployed in 1981, and a programme to integrate the HARM anti-radiation missile with the Intruder is now underway.

Though the totally upgraded A-6F was cancelled in 1988, the A-6E remains in low-rate production, and Boeing Military Airplane Company has developed new graphite/epoxy wings which are being fitted to 102 existing aircraft, and may be fitted to as many as 338. Grumman is fitting these wings to new A-6Es. Grumman converted 78 A-6As into KA-6D tankers, others are rebuilt A-6Es and 49 tankers are being upgraded with five drop tanks but no weapons.

*Right: A final canopy polish and this A-6E will be ready for launch from the catapults of the US Navy's CV-60 Saratoga.*

# Grumman EA-6 Prowler

The first attempt to provide a specialist ECM aircraft for the US Navy was the EA-6A Intruder, a converted A-6A fitted with more than 30 different antennae for monitoring, classifying, recording, jamming and deceiving enemy radar transmissions, but which retained a limited attack capability. The EA-6B Prowler which succeeded it is, however, a completely redesigned aircraft incorporating a very advanced and comprehensive suite of ECM equipment, both internal and podded. Five ALQ-99 high-power tactical jamming pods, each with windmill generators, can be carried, and enemy radar transmissions are monitored and countered by two EW operators seated side by side in the rear. The pilot sits on the left, and on his right is an ECM officer who manages navigation, communications, defensive ECM and the dispensing of chaff. The change from a two-seat to a four-seat configuration has entailed a complete redesign of the forward part of the fuselage, resulting in a longer aircraft than the baseline A-6.

The US Navy has nine electronic warfare squadrons currently in service, each of four aircraft, and

construction continues with a view to providing one squadron for each of the carrier air wings. EA-6Bs also serve alongside older EA-6As in a single Marine Corps ECM squadron.

*Right: All ready to go, and CV-60 Saratoga's catapult officer gives the signal to fire this EA-6B. The nearest underwing store is an active jammer pod.*

*Below: Simulating a low-level attack mission somewhere in the Mediterranean theatre, this EA-6B is carrying three jammer pods and two tanks.*

# Grumman E-2C Hawkeye

The most capable carrier-based airborne early warning (AEW) aircraft yet produced, the E-2C Hawkeye has been offered as an alternative to the more expensive E-3 AWACS to operate from land bases, and a number of aircraft of this type have been purchased by five other customers. In its naval application the E-2C is stationed some 200nm (370km) from the carrier, using its height above sea level to extend the radar horizon of the task force. Hostile aircraft are tracked and fighters of the combat air patrol (CAP) vectored out towards them; the E-2C can also pick up hostile surface units before they enter missile range and direct carrier attack aircraft against them.

The key to the aircraft's mission is the distinctive 24ft (7.3m) diameter saucer-shaped radome for the APS-125 UHF radar, which is mounted above the fuselage. The dome rotates in a free airstream at six revolutions per minute, and can be retracted for hangar stowage aboard the older carriers, reducing height to 16ft (4.87m). The radar can pick up aircraft up to 240nm (444km) away and can track 250 air and surface targets simultaneously. Data are analysed by an on-board computer and the radar picture monitored by three controllers seated at consoles in the Combat Information Centre (CIC), which is located in the fuselage directly beneath the radome. The Airborne Tactical Data System (ATDS) incorporates data links providing real-time communications with the task force or land base.

By 1988 orders amounted to 138, of which 116 had been delivered with the rest following at six per year, those delivered from 1989 having the greatly upgraded APS-145 radar and other changes.

*Above: One of the first Hawkeyes in the early 1960s in formation with the aircraft it replaced, the E-1 Tracer.*

*Below: The current Hawkeye is the E-2C, now being upgraded with yet another new radar. This example has just been launched from CV-60.*

# Grumman F-14 Tomcat

The F-14 Tomcat is the world's most advanced carrier-based fighter. Designed for the Fleet Air Defence role, the Tomcat would operate round-the-clock combat air patrols in conjunction with the E-2C Hawkeye airborne early warning aircraft. The F-14's powerful AWG-9 doppler-pulse fire control radar, which is mounted in the nose of the F-14, can track simultaneously up to 24 targets, plus its own missiles, out to a distance of 60-100nm (111-185km) using track-while-scan techniques. The Phoenix air-to-air missile, unique to this aircraft, incorporates an auto-pilot set by the fire control system as the missile is fired. The target is illuminated only when the missile approaches its target, making countermeasures difficult. Besides its semi-active homing head the missile also incorporates a short-range active radar, so that beyond a certain point the missile homes itself. Medium-range Sparrows and shorter-range infra-red homing (Sidewinder) missiles are also carried for close engagements, and there is a single multi-barrel Vulcan M61 20mm cannon.

The adoption of variable geometry gives good close combat manoeuvrability. The angle of the wings is computer-controlled to obtain the best possible performance in a combat situation; the wings extend for slow-speed landings and long-range flight and retract for high-speed manoeuvring.

Two squadrons each of 12 Tomcats are operated by each of the newer US Navy super-carriers, and since 1981 these have included a detachment of specially-fitted F-14A/TARPS photo-reconnaissance aircraft. The F-14A has replaced the RF-8G Crusader in this role, and carries frame and panoramic cameras and an infra-red line scanner in a pod mounted beneath the fuselage (i.e. in place of the Phoenix missiles); this podded system is designated TARPS (Tactical Air Reconnaissance Pod System).

Though a splendid basic aircraft, which has clearly influenced the latest Soviet fighters, the F-14 has suffered from many deficiencies, by far the most serious being the engines. An early plan to fit P&W F401 engines,

resulting in the F-14B, was cancelled. So bad was the experience with the TF30 that in 1981 the original prototype F-14B was tested with the new General Electric F110 engine, and in 1984 Grumman was awarded a $984 million contract to develop the F-14A .Plus with the GE engine, followed by the F-14D with the GE engine and totally upgraded avionics. Grumman has delivered 38 A Plus aircraft from November 1987, and 32 existing F-14As are being refitted with GE engines. The first of 127 F-14Ds is to be delivered in March 1990, and ultimately Grumman expects to re-manufacture 400 A and A Plus Tomcats to D standard. Apart from having a totally new standard of reliability, the A Plus and D have 20 per cent more specific excess energy for manoeuvres, 60 per cent greater deck-launched intercept radius and 35 per cent greater CAP time on station.

Above: An F-14A thunders away from one of the newer carriers, CVN-68 Nimitz. Ranged on the deck are Vought A-7E Corsair IIs.

Below: Few enemy pilots will ever get this view of a Tomcat! This F-14A is carrying a full complement of AIM-54 Phoenix.

# Kamov Ka-25 Hormone

The Ka-25 Hormone has been the standard Soviet shipborne helicopter since it entered service in the mid-1960s, although it is now being superseded by the Ka-27 Helix. The distinctive co-axial rotor configuration characteristic of nearly all the designs emanating from the Kamov bureau results in excellent lift characteristics in a helicopter of relatively small size, although the height of the Hormone has precluded its operation from smaller surface units.

The Hormone A can accommodate a variety of weapons in an internal weapons bay, and is fitted with a surface search radar (located in a prominent chin radome), a towed MAD and a dunking sonar. Fuel tanks can be fitted externally, and later models of the helicopter have a box housing on the rear fuselage which may be for sonobuoys.

The Hormone B variant is specially fitted to provide mid-course guidance for long-range cruise missiles launched from major surface units. It has a larger chin radome (designated Puff Ball) of a different shape from that of the Hormone A, and there are a number of other differences in the electronics outfit. There appears to be no internal weapons bay.

The Hormone C is a utility helicopter, employed for plane guard, general transport duties and vertical

replenishment (VERTREP). A reconnaissance variant, with a long ventral pannier and camera pod, has also been observed. Hormone Cs generally operate in an all-white colour-scheme which distinguishes them from other models.

*Right: A Ka-25 Hormone-A watching USCG cutter Munro which on 22 September 1983 was searching for wreckage of Korean Airlines Flight 007 (a Boeing 747) which three weeks earlier had been shot down over Soviet territory.*

*Right: Ka-25s operating from Moskva·during this ship's first cruise in 1968. Rope mats are spread over the landing spots.*

# Kamov Ka-27 Helix

The Ka-27 Helix (military version of the Ka-32) was first seen during exercise ZAPAD 81, when two helicopters of the type (one in civilian colours) operated from the new Soviet destroyer *Udaloy*. Although its cabin is larger than that of the Hormone, the Helix is clearly designed to be compatible with ships capable of operating the former. The antisubmarine variant which entered service on *Udaloy* has been designated Helix A. This three-seater has a higher performance than its predecessor and carries a heavier load over much greater radii or

mission endurance. About 80 are in use, plus eight with the Indian Navy. Helix-B is a Marines assault transport, with weapon pylons and different avionics. Helix-C is the civil Ka-32. Helix-D is a comprehensively equipped all-weather SAR (search and rescue) version, with completely new equipment (including external auxiliary tanks and a high-capacity winch).

*Right: An early production Ka-27 parked with blades folded on the destroyer Udaloy during this ship's first foreign cruise in 1982.*

# Lockheed S-3 Viking

Designed to replace the venerable S-2 Tracker in the carrier-borne fixed-wing antisubmarine role, the S-3 Viking is an altogether more sophisticated aircraft equipped with the most advanced detection and data processing capabilities. The major proportion of the Viking's cost is taken up by electronics. Sensors include a high-resolution radar (APS-116), MAD (AQS-81), Forward-Looking Infra-Red (FLIR), and a tube launcher for 60 sonobuoys. The MAD boom, FLIR, and the fuel probe retract into the fuselage to reduce drag. Sensor data are processed by a 65,000-word

AYK-30 digital computer. Behind the pilot and co-pilot, seated side-by-side beneath a broad cockpit, there are consoles for a tactical coordinator and a systems operator.

The initial US Navy production run of 184 aircraft was completed in FY1977. From the mid-1970 fixed-wing ASW squadrons (VS) each of ten S-3A Vikings were added to the air groups of the US super-carriers. Only the two older carriers of the Midway class do not operate the Viking. In spite of some initial criticism directed at the additional maintenance load imposed by the S-3A, its ability to react

quickly and effectively to a distant submarine contact has proved invaluable, and a contract has recently been signed for the upgrading of S-3As to S-3B standard; the latter modification will involve an increase in acoustic and radar processing capabilities, expanded ESM coverage, a new sonobuoy receiver system, and the Harpoon

anti-ship missile. In 1986 the Navy contracted for 22 A/B mod kits, delivered from January 1988, aircraft being converted at Cecil Field, Florida. Altogether 144 aircraft may be converted. Lockheed is also rebuilding 16 aircraft as ES-3A electronic reconnaissance platforms, replacing Skywarriors, and hopes to build 82 or 103 new S-3Bs.

# McDonnell Douglas A-4 Skyhawk

Affectionately known as 'Heinemann's hot-rod' after its designer, Ed. Heinemann, the A-4 Skyhawk began life as a lightweight day nuclear strike aircraft operating from US Navy carriers. Its small size was made possible by the elimination of virtually all electronic equipment. The wing was constructed as a single unit with an integral fuel tank, a folding wing being unnecessary because of the small size of the Skyhawk. Later versions were heavier due to the installation of a more powerful engine, and increases in fuel capacity and payload. All-weather avionics were added in a distinctive dorsal 'hump' from the A-4F onwards. The last model to be built in large numbers was the A-4M. In all 2,960 Skyhawks were built, and the aircraft continued in production for the US Marine Corps until 1979.

The Skyhawk is now used by the US Navy only for training, but the Marine Corps still has four light attack squadrons (VMA) each with 19 A-4Ms;

these will be replaced in the near future by the AV-8B Harrier II. Seventy A-4P Skyhawks (converted A-4B/C) were purchased by the Argentine Air Force from 1966 onwards and were employed extensively on maritime strike missions during the Falklands conflict of 1982. This is particularly well documented, with both the Argentinian Navy and Air Force operating A-4s entirely from shore bases, with in-flight refuelling often being a vital ingredient in successful missions. Of the 50 A-4s available at the start of the conflict 22 did not return. The Argentine Navy also purchased 16 A-4Q Skyhawks in 1971 for operation from the carrier 25 de Mayo. The Australian Navy purchased eight new A-4G Skyhawks in 1967 for the carrier Melbourne, and a similar number of ex-US A-4Gs in 1971.

*Above: The first of 179 production S-3As on trials in 1973. Lockheed studied over 12 derived versions for other missions.*

*Below: The compact carrier-based S-3A (which folds into an even smaller space) is here seen with the much bigger shore-based P-3C.*

*Below: Two-seat TA-4J Skyhawks used by US Navy squadron VA-127 for Aggressor training. The Navy also uses the F-16N, and Kfirs.*

# McDonnell Douglas (BAe) AV-8 Harrier

One hundred and ten AV-8A Harriers, based on the RAF's GR.3 but modified to US Marine Corps specifications, were built in the UK under contract from McDonnell Douglas between 1971 and 1977. In 1975 Spain ordered six AV-8Ss (re-christened Matador) plus two TAV-8S trainers for VTOL operations from the carrier *Dédalo*, and a further five were delivered in 1980.

The Marine Corps aircraft differed from their RAF counterparts in being fitted from the outset to carry AIM-9 Sidewinder AAMs on the outer pylons for the air defence role, and it was the Marines who introduced the practice of VIFFing (= vectoring in forward flight) in close combat. The best 47 USMC aircraft have been converted to AV-8C standard with updated EW systems, flare/chaff dispenser, a lift-improvement system, new communications and on-board oxygen generation. The employment of a short rolling take-off, vertical landing (STOVL) mode of operations enables more than 5,000lb (2,270kg) of bombs to be carried.

Only superficially similar, the AV-8B Harrier II now in production has a graphite/epoxy wing of new design, Angle/Rate Bombing System, totally new cockpit, 25mm five-barrel gun and pylons for up to 17,000lb (7,711kg) of external weapons which can be delivered with pinpoint accuracy. In early 1988 the 100th of a planned 323 (295 plus 28 TAV-8B trainers) was delivered to the US Marines. The Spanish Navy has received 12 EAV-8Bs. Britain's RAF uses a land-based version with several significant differences.

*Above: AV-8A Harriers of Marine Corps squadron VMA-513 landing aboard LHA-1 Tarawa at anchor in San Diego harbour.*

*Below: Pilot-production AV-8B makes free rolling takeoff in 1984. By 1989 the AV-8B will equip the three Fleet AV-8A units plus five A-4 squadrons.*

## McDonnell Douglas F/A-18 Hornet

The original requirement for the F/A-18 came as a result of the escalating costs of the F-14 Tomcat programme. In 1974 specifications for a new, smaller fighter designated VFAX were drawn up, and in 1975 the US Navy and the Marine Corps chose the F-18, developed by McDonnell Douglas and Northrop from the experimental YF-17. The need to reduce maintenance requirements aboard the carriers, the air groups of which were now to receive fixed-wing ASW squadrons in addition to their fighter and attack squadrons, resulted in the F-18 being given a dual interceptor/light attack role. This in turn brought an increase in weight and power over the original design. Costs have also rocketed, and the F/A-18 is now as expensive as the F-14 itself.

The Hornet has a very advanced

array of cockpit displays which enables it to dispense with the second crewman — a feature which has attracted some criticism. Special attention has been given to increasing reliability. Conversion from fighter to attack configuration, and vice-versa, will be a simple operation involving only the replacement of pods and weapons; all aircraft have the same APG-65 radar and air/ground sensors. It was originally envisaged that the Hornet would replace the F-4 Phantom in six Navy and nine Marine fighter attack squadrons, the A-4 Skyhawk and AV-8A Harrier in seven Marine light attack squadrons, and

*Below: The first F/A-18 unit to go to sea was test unit VX-5, which operated from CV-64 Constellation in October 1982.*

the A-7 Corsair in 24 Navy light attack squadrons, but decisions to proceed with the AV-8B Harrier for the USMC and to continue F-14 Tomcat production for the Navy means that the F/A-18 will now replace only the Marine Phantoms and the Navy's

Corsairs. The first aircraft were delivered in 1981, and today over 600 are in service, current F/A-18C (two-seat -18D) aircraft having major avionics updates and carrying six AMRAAMs or four IR-imaging Mavericks.

## Sikorsky SH-3 Sea King

The SH-3 Sea King, which entered service more than 25 years ago, remains the standard carrier-based ASW helicopter in service with the US Navy and other navies.

The earliest ASW model, the SH-3A, was operated from the antisubmarine carriers of the Essex class. A total of 255 were built for the US Navy, and the SH-3A served as the basis for 41 CH-124s (ex-CHSS-2) built under licence by United Aircraft of Canada, and 73 S-61Bs (ex-HSS-2) built under licence by Mitsubishi for the JMSDF. Twelve of the US Navy models were converted as SAR helicopters with armament and armour, and became HH-3As. A further 105 were converted as utility helicopters and became SH-3Gs. From 1966 the SH-3A was superseded in production by the SH-3D, of

which 72 were built for the US Navy, 22 for Spain and four for Brazil. Four similar S-61Ds were purchased by Argentina, and Agusta of Italy built 24 under licence for the Italian Navy, and seven for Iran; a follow-up order of 30 for the Italian Navy was placed in the late 1970s. The current SH-3H variant in service with the US Navy is a multi-purpose version of the SH-3G, with new ASW equipment. All remaining SH-3A and SH-3D models are being updated to -3H standard, and the last ASH-3H batch produced by Agusta can carry Marte 2, Exocet or Harpoon missiles.

*Below: Denmark's 722 Sqn, based at Vaerlose, flies the S-61A in the SAR mission. British Sea Kings are made by Westland.*

## Sikorsky CH-53 Sea Stallion and Super Stallion

The Ch-53 Sea Stallion is a heavy assault helicopter developed specifically for the US Marine Corps. It is a hybrid combining an enlarged Sea King fuselage and the six-bladed rotor and power train systems of the Army's CH-54 Skycrane helicopter. It can carry 38 fully-armed troops, with an alternative loading of two jeeps, two Hawk missiles or a 105mm howitzer, embarked via a rear-loading ramp. Delivery of the CH-53A began in 1966, with the improved CH-53D following in 1969. A total of 265 of both variants were built, and the Marine Corps operates seven helicopter squadrons each with 15-21 CH-53A/D, which provide LPH/LHA detachments.

The RH-53D mine countermeasures variant is operated by the US Navy. It is a basic CH-53A/D with upgraded engines (T64-GE-415), a strengthened fuselage, an automatic flight control system, and attachment points for a variety of MCM devices (Mk 103 mechanical, Mk 104 acoustic, Mk 105 magnetic, and Mk 106 magnetic/acoustic). The first Navy

MCM squadron was equipped with 15 modified CH-53As, but 30 new-built RH-53Ds were delivered from September 1973, and three squadrons, each of 4-7 helicopters, are now operational. Six additional RH-53Ds were delivered to Iran.

The CH-53E Super Stallion is a three-engine heavy-lift derivative for Navy and USMC use. It can lift a massive 16 tons (50 per cent more than the CH-47 Chinook), a figure which accounts for 93 per cent of all heavy equipment in service with a Marine division. In the aircraft recovery role all current Navy and USMC types can be carried. By early 1988 over 100 CH-53Es had been delivered to the Marines and Navy, including the specialised MH-53E Sea Dragon MCM (mine countermeasures version) with giant side tanks and able to tow any kind of sweeping gear.

*Right: The MH-53E is visibly distinguished by its huge fuel tanks on each side. The pull on the mine-sweeping gear can exceed 16 tons.*

## Sikorsky SH-60 Seahawk

Since 1974 the US Navy has standardised on two versions of the basic S-70 family (the first member of which was the Army UH-60A Black Hawk). Chronologically the first to enter service was the SH-60B Seahawk, an ASW (anti-submarine warfare) machine operated from destroyers and frigates. Large, costly and very well equipped, 204 are being delivered, plus others for Japan, Spain and Australia.

In 1988 the go-ahead was given for the SH-60F or CV-Helo. To be based aboard the Navy's carriers, this version is replacing the SH-3H Sea King to protect the inner zone of a carrier battle group against submarine attack. In many ways the SH-60F is simplified, the basic ASW suite of radar, pneumatic sonobuoy launchers and many other devices being removed, together with the system for recovering on a pitching ship deck. Instead this version has a dipping sonar, as well as a MAD, FLIR, ESM and many new devices, as well as the new Mk 50 torpedoes. A

secondary role is plane-guard duty and SAR (search and rescue) missions. The Navy will receive 175, beginning in 1989. The Navy and US Coast Guard are also buying HH-60 Rescue Hawk versions for combat rescue and special warfare tasks.

With a four-hour mission endurance (at a temperature of 90°F at sea level and no-wind OGE — Out of Ground Effect — hover), the SH-60F has the ability to meet the double-deck cyclic operations carrier schedule, while carrying a full load of stores.

The European company Rolls-Royce Turbomeca hoped to power these later versions with a brilliant new engine, the RTM322. Despite outstanding performance and reliability demonstrated in an SH-60B the Navy decided in 1988 to stick with the American T700 engine.

*Right: The 25 sonobuoy launch tubes stand out prominently from the low-vis grey of the SH-60B, which is too big for most frigates.*

## LTV (Vought) A-7 Corsair II

The A-7 Corsair was developed as a replacement for the A-4 Skyhawk in the day attack rôle. A simple, robust, lightweight aircraft with minimal avionics was specified. Vought proposed an adaptation of the successful F-8 Crusader interceptor, and the adoption of this proposal helped to speed development and delivery. By restricting performance to high subsonic — the F-8 Crusader was capable of Mach 1.7 — structure weight was reduced, range dramatically increased and weapon load quadrupled.

One hundred and ninety-nine A-7As were built, closely followed by 196 A-7Bs. Later models incorporated the customary improvements in avionics to provide a limited all-weather and night capability. In 1966 the Corsair was adopted by the US Air Force, resulting in an improved A-7D model with the more powerful T41 engine, a multi-barrel M61 Vulcan 20mm cannon, and all-weather avionics. The US Navy subsequently adopted the same model with an uprated T41 engine, and 596 A-7Es were delivered. Production was ended in 1983 in favour of the F/A-18 Hornet. In 1981-83 the Navy bought 91 FLIR (Forward-Looking Infra-Red) pods and 231 FLIR installations, the latter including new Marconi HUDs for improved night capability.

*Below: A-7Es of US Navy squadron VA-81 Sunliners getting ready for the day's work aboard Saratoga.*

## Vought F-8 Crusader

The F-8 Crusader began life as a carrier-based day fighter with the US Navy. It was the first production aircraft capable of speeds in excess of 1,000mph, and proved extremely manoeuvrable. A total of 1,261 Crusaders were built, and the aircraft remained in service as an interceptor aboard the smaller US attack carriers well into the 1970s. A photo-reconnaissance model was introduced in the early stages of the aircraft's development. Three plane detachments of rebuilt RF-8Gs remained in service aboard the big super-carriers into the early 1980s.

The small size of the Crusader made it the only suitable high-performance jet fighter available when the French light fleet carriers *Clemenceau* and *Foch* were completed in the early 1960s and 42 F-8Es were purchased in 1963 for delivery in 1966. A number of special modifications were necessary to enable the Crusader to operate from the French carriers. These included the replacement of the radar by one compatible with the Matra R.530 missile, and modifications to the airframe (double aileron and flap deflection, enlarged tail surfaces, and a reduction in travel of the variable-incidence wing) aimed at reducing the landing speed by some 15kt (28km/h).

*Below: With wing tilted up, an F-8E(FN) is ready for launch. There will be a gap between retirement of F-8s and arrival of Rafale.*

## Yakovlev Yak-38 Forger

A prototype Soviet VTOL aircraft, the Yak-36 Freehand, went on public display in 1967. It had two turbojets side by side, with a ram inlet in the nose, exhausting through two large gridded vectored nozzles. When the production Yak-38 finally emerged aboard the ASW cruiser *Kiev* in 1976, however, it became clear that considerable redesign work had taken place during the development phase.

The Forger has a multi-engine configuration, with two small vertical lift jets complementing a single main vectored-thrust turbojet. The vertical lift jets improve stability in the delicate take-off and landing phases, but at the cost of higher fuel consumption (with a consequent reduction in range) and loss of the aircraft in the event of any engine failure. Short rolling take-offs permit an increased payload.

The Forger appears to have been developed initially as an interceptor, to protect Soviet surface forces from air attack and to shoot down hostile reconnaissance and LRMP aircraft. However, the limited endurance and performance of the Forger, together with the lack of AEW aircraft aboard the Soviet ASW cruisers, considerably reduces its effectiveness in this role. It is also employed as a close support aircraft, or for short-range surface strike against minor surface vessels. A number of two-seat Forger B trainers have also been observed.

*Right: Yak-38s lashed down aboard the Minsk. Operations appear to rely on precision guidance from the parent vessel.*

# Index

Page numbers in **bold** type refer to subjects mentioned in captions to illustrations